Reading Group Choices

*Selections for Lively
Book Discussions*

Paz & Associates

2003

© 2002 Paz & Associates
All Rights Reserved.
Published in the United States by Paz & Associates.

For further information, contact:
Mark Kaufman, Editor
Reading Group Choices

Paz & Associates
800/260-8605 — phone
mkaufman@pazbookbiz.com — email

Visit our websites at:
www.readinggroupchoices.com
www.pazbookbiz.com

ISBN 0-9644876-8-3

Cover design: Gena Kennedy

Printed by:
Boyd Brothers, Inc.
425 East 15th St.
Panama City, FL 32405
850/763-1741

CONTENTS

CONTENTS (continued)

INTRODUCTION

The selections in this year's edition will introduce you to some fascinating and unforgettable characters, transport you to distant times and places, and elevate your spirit—often all within the pages of one book!

That's the absolute joy and wonder of a great read—both satisfying and nourishing you in ways that no other media can. In these trying economic times, we may have cut back on everything from travel to entertainment, but there's still the power of an affordable book—the best investment you can make.

In this ninth edition of *Reading Group Choices*, you'll find book group favorites like **The Lovely Bones, The Amazing Adventures of Kavalier & Clay,** and **Peace Like a River,** as well as some classics and first novels that have potential to become favorites in the future.

There are Pulitzer Prize winners, like **Michael Chabon** and **Eugene O'Neill**, bestselling authors like **Amy Tan** and **Anne Lamott**, and authors whose latest novels are every bit as wonderful as their first, like **Tracy Chevalier**, **Rohinton Mistry**, and **Niall Williams**. And you'll meet authors like **Sigrid Undset**, whose spirit lives on long after her passing.

Unlike a number of the dark and disturbing titles that were Oprah picks, you'll find within these pages an assortment for every mood and every occasion. Those who like to look back in time will especially enjoy **Year of Wonders, The Fall of Light**, and **In Paterson**. Fans of page-turners that keep you in suspense will like **The Lake of Dead Languages**, **Not the End of the World**, and **The Gospel of Judas**. Seekers of personal growth should note **The Buddha in Your Mirror** and **The Raven Who Spoke With God**. And those who enjoy a good chuckle as they read will delight in **Ella Minnow Pea** and **The Miracle Life of Edgar Mint**.

One thing is certain—whether you're discussing family relationships, the nature of love, the immigrant experience, race relations, or the very state of the world, these selections will not only fill your time, but your hearts and minds as well. Enjoy!

Mark Kaufman and **Donna Paz**

October, 2002

P.S. The votes have been counted … book group favorites, chosen by visitors to our web site, include **The Red Tent, Girl With a Pearl Earring, The Poisonwood Bible, Pope Joan,** and more. For a complete listing, see **www.readinggroupchoices.com**.

About Paz & Associates
and *Reading Group Choices*

One of the goals of Paz & Associates is to join with publishers and bookstores to develop resources and skills that promote books and reading. We offer a variety of products and services to bookstores, publishers, and other book-related organizations, including the following:

- consulting with prospective and current retail booksellers on marketing, human resources, store design, merchandising, and business operations, including financial analysis, buying and inventory management

- *The Reader's Edge* bookstore newsletter marketing program

- *Opening a Bookstore: The Essential Planning Guide*

- *Opening a Bookstore: The Business Essentials*, 5-day intensive workshops (see web site for dates and locations)

- *The Training Guide to FrontLine Bookselling*

- Training Videos *Exceptional FrontLine Bookselling: It's All About Service,* and *Bookstore Merchandising Made Easy*

Reading Group Choices is distributed annually to bookstores, libraries, and directly to book groups. Titles from previous issues are posted on our website at **www.readinggroupchoices.com.** Books presented here have been recommended by book group members, librarians, booksellers, literary agents, publicists, authors, and publishers. All submissions are then reviewed to ensure the "discussibility" of each title. Once a title is approved for inclusion, publishers are then asked to underwrite production costs, so that copies of **Reading Group Choices** can be distributed for a minimal charge.

For additional copies, please call your local library or bookstore, or you may contact us by phone or email as shown below. We will be happy to ship copies to you directly, or let you know of a bookstore or library in your area that has obtained copies of **Reading Group Choices**. Quantities are limited. For more information, please visit our websites at **www.readinggroupchoices.com** and **www.pazbookbiz.com.**

Paz & Associates

800/260-8605 ◆ dpaz@pazbookbiz.com

ACKNOWLEDGMENTS

We wish to thank the authors, agents, publicists, and our publishing colleagues who have continued to support this publication by calling to our attention some quality books for group discussion:

Authorlink Press	Ballantine Books
Donna Woolfolk Cross	Elton-Wolf Publishing
Grove/Atlantic	HarperCollins
Hyperion Books	Alfred A. Knopf
Louisiana State University Press	Middleway Press
Penguin/Putnam Publishing Group	Picador (St. Martin's Press)
Singing Spirit Books	SMU Press (Miriam Levine)
Spinsters Ink	Steerforth Press
Time Warner Book Group	Vintage Books (Random House)
Westcliffe Publishers	Yale University Press

In appreciation of an ongoing alliance with Paz & Associates and *Reading Group Choices*, we especially thank graphic designer **Gena Kennedy** for her artwork and production expertise.

THE AMAZING ADVENTURES OF KAVALIER & CLAY

Author: Michael Chabon

Publisher: Picador USA, 2001

Website: www.picadorusa.com

Available in:
Paperback, 639 pages. $15.00
(ISBN 0-312-28299-0)

Genre: Fiction/Pop Culture/
Jewish Interest

Summary

Joe Kavalier, a young Jewish artist who has also been trained in the art of Houdiniesque escape, has just smuggled himself out of Nazi-invaded Prague and landed in New York City. His Brooklyn cousin Sammy Clay is looking for a partner to create heroes, stories, and art for the latest novelty to hit America—the comic book. Drawing on their own fears and dreams, Kavalier and Clay create the Escapist, the Monitor, and Luna Moth, inspired by the beautiful Rosa Saks, who will become linked by powerful ties to both men. With exhilarating style and grace, Michael Chabon tells an unforgettable story about American romance and possibility.

Recommended by: *The Washington Post Book World*

"Absolutely gosh-wow, super-colossal—smart, funny, and a continual pleasure to read."

Author Biography

Michael Chabon is the bestselling author of *Werewolves in Their Youth*, *Wonder Boys*, *A Model World and Other Stories*, and *The Mysteries of Pittsburgh*. He lives in California with his wife and children. *The Amazing Adventures of Kavalier and Clay* won the Bay Area Book Reviewer's Award and the New York Society Library Award, and was a finalist for the PEN/Faulkner Award, the National Book Critics Circle Award, and the *Los Angeles Times* Book Award.

Topics to Consider

1) What does the portrayal of Sammy Klayman suggest about growing up in urban America in the late 1930s?

2) What is the appeal of Houdini to Sammy and Joe? How is that appeal common to boys growing up during the depression? To boys of any era?

3) The theme of escape runs throughout the novel. What are Sammy and Joe escaping from? What are they escaping to?

4) What role does the Golem have in the story? What does the Golem signify? Why did Chabon include this legend in his novel?

5) What is a superhero? Are superhero stories mythological in nature? What is it about the experience of young men that inspires superhero stories?

6) In what ways are the experiences of Joe Kavalier parallel to the events in the Superman myth?

7) How does Rosa represent stability and security in the novel? Is she in control of her own destiny, or is she subject to the needs and whims of the men in her life? Is there anything that she is escaping from or to?

8) What is the significance of names and name-changes in the novel? How are names significant in the legend of the Golem?

9) How are Joe Kavalier's life and longings reflected in his fictional hero the Escapist?

10) Sammy has a relationship with an actor named Tracy Bacon. What is the attraction between the two men? How does Tracy—in name and person—represent a forbidden fruit to Sammy?

11) How was Joe's escape from Czechoslovakia mirrored in his survival at the Antarctic Naval station? In what ways were these two escapes similar? What did Bernard Kornblum represent in each case?

Additional topics for discussion can be found at www.picadorusa.com.

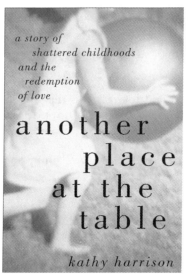

ANOTHER PLACE AT THE TABLE

Author: Kathy A. Harrison

Publisher: Tarcher/Putnam, 4/2003

Website: www.penguinputnam.com

Available in:
Hardcover, 329 pages. $23.95
(ISBN 1-58542-200-2)

Genre: Nonfiction/Memoir/
Parenting/Love

Summary

Kathy Harrison describes her experiences as a foster parent to abandoned babies, runway teens, preschoolers in wheelchairs, ten-year-old girls just discharged from psychiatric hospitals, and others so physically and emotionally damaged that most adults would run the other way rather than spend two minutes with them. Knowing there is only so much she can do, she also knows that she is, at least for a brief time, providing these children with the only comfort and safety they have known in their short lives. For anyone who cares about children, families, and the future of our fragile country, **Another Place at the Table** is the chronicle of a woman whose best intentions for a child are sometimes all that stands between redemption and violence.

Recommended by: *Boston Globe Magazine*

"Bad foster homes grab headlines. Good ones don't but each of them has a story— complicated, demanding, and full of its own kind of hard-won love. Kathy and Bruce Harrison represent the best that foster care can offer."

Author Biography

Kathy Harrison has been a foster parent for over thirteen years, hosting almost a hundred children. In 1996, she and her husband Bruce were named Massachusetts Foster Parents of the Year, and in 2002, they received the prestigious Goldie Foster Award for Foster Parents. A frequent public speaker, Harrison lives near Northampton, Massachusetts with her family—three biological sons, three adoptive daughters, and a constantly changing cast of foster children.

Topics to Consider

1) Before you read this book, did you ever think much about foster parents and foster children and the foster care system in general? Were your impressions of all three negative, positive, or neutral?

2) Harrison writes about the many negative stereotypes about foster parents and foster children. Do you ever find yourself thinking in terms of those stereotypes? What keeps them alive?

3) Did any one child in Harrison's book touch you the most? What was it about his/her story that touched you?

4) What parts of Harrison's book surprised or disturbed you the most?

5) When you were a child, did you have a non-parent adult in your life who helped you through a tough time, propped you up, mentored you, loved and encouraged you, or otherwise had a positive impact?

6) As an adult, have you ever helped a child (not your own) in the above ways? Do you feel that you made a difference in that child's life?

7) There are half a million children in the foster care system. In Harrison's view, it is an imperfect, financially depleted, and overburdened system. What do you think is the solution? Do you feel that our government should spend more money on social services? Or do you feel that our tax dollars are better spent in other areas?

8) Harrison talks about having long conversations in her head telling birth mothers what to do. Do you ever have those conversations in your head with parents you know? As you read Harrison's book, did you ever find yourself passing judgment on *her* parenting skills?

9) When is it appropriate to keep our opinions to ourselves about other people's parenting, and when is it appropriate to speak up? Of course one should intervene if there is serious abuse going on. But what about the gray areas, such as when we see another parent screaming at a child, spanking a child, or acting out (with sexual behavior, booze, etc.) in front of a child? Where do *you* draw the line?

10) Do you ever imagine yourself becoming a foster parent? What would be the positive aspects of it for you? What would be the negative aspects?

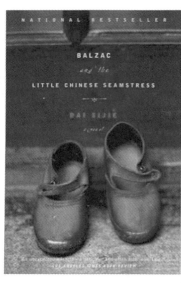

BALZAC AND THE LITTLE CHINESE SEAMSTRESS

Author: Dai Sijie

Publisher: Anchor Books, 2002

Website: www.vintagebooks.com/read

Available in:
Paperback, 192 pages, $10.00
(ISBN 0-385-72220-6)

Genre: Fiction/Literature/
Chinese Culture

Summary

Balzac and the Little Chinese Seamstress is an enchanting tale that captures the magic of reading and the wonder of romantic awakening. An immediate international bestseller, it tells the story of two hapless city boys exiled to a remote mountain village for re-education during China's infamous Cultural Revolution. There the two friends meet the daughter of the local tailor and discover a hidden stash of Western classics in Chinese translation. As they flirt with the seamstress and secretly devour these banned works, the two friends find transit from their grim surroundings to worlds they never imagined.

Recommended by: *Los Angeles Times Book Review*

"An unexpected miracle ... a delicate, and often hilarious tale."

Author Biography

Born in China in 1954, **Dai Sijie** is a filmmaker who was re-educated during the Cultural Revolution. In 1984 he left China for France, where he has lived and worked ever since. *Balzac and the Little Chinese Seamstress*, his first novel, was an overnight sensation when it was published in France in 2000, becoming an immediate bestseller and winning five prizes. Rights to the novel have been sold in nineteen countries, and it is soon to be made into a film.

Topics to Consider

1) What does **Balzac and the Little Chinese Seamstress** reveal about the nature and purpose of China's Cultural Revolution and the suffering it caused?

2) Why have the narrator's and Luo's parents been named "enemies of the people"? What were their crimes? How does this classification affect the fate of the two boys? Why did China want to reeducate people like the narrator and Luo?

3) Is the narrator right about the marginal status of the storyteller in the modern world [p. 18]? In what ways is this novel an argument for the importance of storytelling?

4) The narrator reads *Ursule Mirouet* [p. 57]. What is it that enables him to identify so strongly with characters and situations he has never experienced? What does his experience suggest about the power of literature? In what ways does **Balzac and the Little Chinese Seamstress** exert a similar power on its readers?

5) Luo is sent to the mountains to be reeducated, an experience he bitterly resents, and yet he himself wishes to reeducate the Seamstress [p. 100]. What is the ironic result of his success in making the Little Seamstress more sophisticated? What does the novel suggest about attempting to change others according to one's own beliefs or desires?

6) When the narrator sees the books in Four Eyes' suitcase [p. 99], and when Luo later burns the novels, it is the characters, rather than the books, that seem to go up in flames. Why does he regard these books as being so alive?

7) As in a harshly realistic novel, the two main characters are forced to work in a coal mine and to carry buckets of excrement up and down a mountain, yet the story also has a fairy-tale quality. What makes the book read like a fable? How has Dai Sijie managed to merge these two narrative traditions?

8) How does the ending—when the Little Seamstress sets off for the city—complicate the novel's apparent endorsement of cosmopolitan Western culture and literature over rural Chinese culture?

For a complete Reading Group Guide,
visit www.vintagebooks.com/read

BLUE SHOE

Author: Anne Lamott

Publisher: Riverhead Books, 2002

Website: www.penguinputnam.com

Available in:
Hardcover, 291 pages. $24.95
(ISBN: 1-57322-226-7)

Genre: Fiction/Family Life/Love

Summary

Mattie Ryder is a marvelously funny, well-intentioned, religious, sarcastic, tender, angry, and broke recently divorced mother of two young children. Then she finds a small rubber blue shoe—the kind you might get from a gumball machine—and a few other trifles that were left years ago in her deceased father's car. They seem to hold the secrets to her messy upbringing, and as she and her brother follow these clues to uncover the mystery of their past, she begins to open her heart to her difficult, brittle mother and the father she thought she knew. And with that acceptance comes an opening up to the possibilities of romantic love.

Recommended by: *The New Yorker*

"Anne Lamott is a cause for celebration. [Her] real genius lies in capturing the ineffable, describing not perfect moments, but imperfect ones ... perfectly. She is nothing short of miraculous."

Author Biography

Anne Lamott is the author of the national bestsellers ***Traveling Mercies***, ***Bird by Bird***, and ***Operating Instructions***, as well as five novels, including ***Crooked Little Heart*** and ***Rosie***. Her column in *Salon* magazine was voted the Best of the Web by *Newsweek* magazine, and she is a past recipient of a Guggenheim Fellowship. She lives in Northern California.

Topics to Consider

1) Consider the blue shoe. What does it mean to each person who carries it—Alfred, Mattie, Daniel, Noah, and Ella? Discuss it in reference to what Mattie remembers reading about children of the Holocaust.

2) Why is Isa such a hero to others, while her daughter feels deprived? Are Mattie's feelings of neglect justified? Do you think Isa was a devoted or neglectful mother to Alfred?

3) What impact did Alfred's behavior have on Mattie and Al as children and on who they are as adults, even though they did not learn the details about his life until they were adults?

4) The light, or its absence, affects Mattie's moods, and she is continually lighting candles or adjusting the light. Discuss the meaning behind the story's references to light and shadow, to seasons changing.

5) Isa lived knowing that her husband loved another woman, who was the same age as her own child. What effect did her husband's "wandering" have on Isa's life? Do you think his infidelity shaped who she was to Mattie and Al? If so, how?

6) Why does Mattie continue to have sex with Nicky after their divorce? Does sleeping with him kill her desire to get back together with him, as she suggests [p. 59]? Or does she need to fill the holes of her childhood with some form of affection, even if it is the wrong kind?

7) How does Mattie's attempt to be someone else affect her relationship with William? How does her honesty with Daniel affect their relationship?

8) Mattie takes great pride in winning Daniel away from Pauline. What does being picked mean to Mattie? Does it make her feel superior to Isa? Is there some vindication here for her own father's lying to her?

9) Discuss the role of faith in Mattie's life: faith in friends, faith in God, faith in family, faith in herself. Does it bring her the acceptance and the love that she feels are missing in other parts of her life? How is her faith tested, and how rewarded, in the novel?

A reading guide is available at www.penguinputnam.com/guides

THE BONE WEAVER

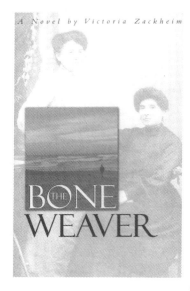

Author: Victoria Zackheim

Publisher: Elton-Wolf Publishing, 2001

Website: www.theboneweaver.com

Available in:
Paperback, 264 pages. $18.98
(ISBN 1-58619-021-0)

Genre: Fiction/Women's Issues/
Relationships/Personal Challenges

Summary

Following the death of her lifelong friend, professor Mimi Zilber sets off on a journey to discover how she came to this lonely place in her life, and why she is running from the opportunity to love. The Bone Weaver is a blend of history and fiction created around three generations of women and their struggles to survive pogroms, illness and the violence of shtetl life in 19th century Europe. By taking apart the family tapestry thread by thread, and then studying these women and their daily lives of uncertainty, tragedy, and joy, Mimi learns important lessons about courage and the will to survive. And in her discovery of what makes these women remarkable, she also discovers herself.

Recommended by: *The Midwest Book Review*

*"...a superbly written generational story...*The Bone Weaver *is a unique, powerful, moving, inspiring, and very highly recommended novel."*

Author Biography

Victoria Zackheim is a San Francisco-based writer who earns her living in marketing communications and corporate/political speech writing, and her gratification from writing fiction and theater.

> **SPECIAL OFFER:** The author will chat online or by telephone with any reading group that selects this book. Interested groups should contact the author at www.theboneweaver.com.

Topics to Consider

1) How would you describe Mimi's reaction to Sarah's death?

2) If you were in Mimi's position, how would you handle Rivka differently?

3) Discuss a point in the novel when your feelings about Mimi change.

4) Discuss a point in the novel when your feelings about Rivka change.

5) Why do you think Mimi is so uncomfortable in her relationships?

6) What are your feelings about the relationship between Mimi and Daniel throughout the novel?

7) If you were Daniel, how would you react to Mimi?

8) In your opinion, who was the central character in this novel?

9) Discuss one scene in the novel that you found memorable.

10) If you could rewrite the last chapter, what would happen between Daniel and Mimi?

THE BONESETTER'S DAUGHTER

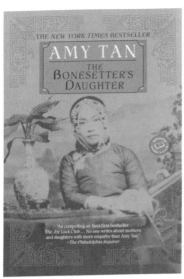

Author: Amy Tan

Publisher: Ballantine Books, 2/2003

Website:
www.ballantinebooks.com/BRC

Available in:
Paperback, 432 pages. $14.95
(ISBN 0-345-45737-4)

Genre: Fiction/Chinese Culture/
Mother-Daughter Relationships

Summary

Here is a story of a Chinese immigrant mother, her American daughter, and the past that binds them together even as it separates them. As a child, Ruth Young was constantly subjected to her mother's disturbing notions about curses and ghosts and to her repeated threats to kill herself. But now LuLing Young seems happy—far from her usual disagreeable and dissatisfied self. LuLing begins to write all that she can remember of her life as a girl in China. When Ruth discovers the papers, she is transported to a backwoods village known as Immortal Heart. Each page reveals secrets of the mute nursemaid, Precious Auntie, and of the curse that LuLing believes she released through betrayal. Within LuLing's pages, written in Chinese, awaits the truth about a mother's heart that she cannot tell her daughter, yet hopes she will never forget.

Recommended by: *People*

"... This book sings with emotion and insight."

Author Biography

Amy Tan is the author of *The Joy Luck Club*, *The Kitchen God's Wife*, *The Hundred Secret Senses*, and two children's books, *The Moon Lady* and *The Chinese Siamese Cat*. Tan was also the co-producer and co-screenwriter of the film version of *The Joy Luck Club*, and her essays and stories have appeared in numerous magazines and anthologies. Her work has been translated into more than twenty-five languages. She lives with her husband in San Francisco and New York.

Topics to Consider

1) What is the significance of the book's title? How does breaking a bone change Ruth's life and her relationship with her mother? What importance do bones hold for LuLing and Precious Auntie?

2) Each year, Ruth makes a conscious decision not to speak for one week. Why does she elect to go silent? How does Ruth find her voice as the novel goes on?

3) LuLing begins her story, "These are the things I must forget." Why does she choose to muffle the past? In which ways did Precious Auntie hide the truth from her? How does Ruth grapple with the hidden past of her family, and what it means for her future?

4) Ruth is shocked to learn that her aunt, GaoLing, is not her mother's real sister. How does the relationship between the two women defy the adage that blood is thicker than water?

5) How does the concept of destiny shape the lives of both Precious Auntie and LuLing? How does each woman fight against the strictures of fate? In the modern world, does destiny hold as much weight? Why or why not?

6) How does Ruth's concept of love differ from that of her grandmother's and mother's? Does LuLing's conception of love evolve over time?

7) How does LuLing forge a new life for herself in America? In which ways does she remain constrained by the past, and in which ways does she triumph over it?

8) As LuLing loses her memory, how does her story become more clear to Ruth? How does Tan explore the transience of memory in *The Bonesetter's Daughter?*

9) What significance do names and their nuances have in this story? Why is it so important that Ruth discover her family's true name? When Ruth discovers what her own name means, how does that realization change her relationship with LuLing?

Additional topics for discussion can be found at
www.ballantinebooks.com/BRC

THE BUDDHA IN YOUR MIRROR

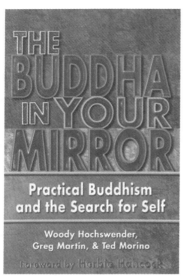

Authors: Woody Hochswender,
Greg Martin & Ted Morino

Publisher: Middleway Press, 2001

Website: www.middlewaypress.org

Available in:
Paperback, 230 pages. $14.00
(ISBN 0-9674697-8-3)

Genre: Nonfiction/
Personal Growth/Religion

Summary

This bestselling Buddhist primer reveals the most modern, effective and practical way to achieve what is called enlightenment or Buddhahood—just as you are, without changing how you look, eat or live. Based on the centuries-old teaching of the Japanese religious reformer Nichiren, this method has been called the "direct path" to enlightenment. One of the most popular forms of Buddhism in the United States, it is embraced by more than 12 million people worldwide. Open to the first page and begin the great adventure—the incredible journey of understanding and discovery that will lead you to your highest self.

Recommended by: *NAPRA Review*

"An excellent introduction to the not-so-new, pragmatic practice that is cropping up all over the Western world: aware of it or not, this is how we are beginning to live. Highly applicable to everyday situations ..."

Author Biographies

Woody Hochswender is a former reporter for the *New York Times* and a former senior editor at *Esquire* magazine. He has been practicing Nichiren Buddhism for more than 25 years and has written two previous books and numerous articles on various topics. **Greg Martin** is a vice general director of the SGI-USA, the lay organization of Nichiren Buddhists in the United States. **Ted Morino** is a vice general director of SGI-USA and is currently editor-in-chief of the organization's weekly newspaper and monthly magazine.

Topics to Consider

1) Thinking of your own mentors or significant others, can you recall a critical message you may have received at some time in your life that allowed you to look at things differently and to grow in your awareness of the world around you?

2) The authors suggest, "Buddhism has no conflict with the world of science." (Page 4) Are the perspectives of faith and science merging in Western society? In what ways?

3) Buddhism and Western religion have differing perspectives. What were the beliefs you grew up with that influenced your self-perception of wisdom and holiness? If you've unlearned or relearned any of those beliefs, discuss the catalyst for that transition.

4) If "every individual is connected to everything on earth" (page 27), how would individuals behave differently in a world where this belief is shared—and lived—by all? What gets in our way of living this belief?

5) The authors say that the underlying aim of this book is world peace (page 29), a result of the process of individual enlightenment and dialogue. Think of people you've known or know of who were living examples of personal enlightenment. How did they influence and/or encourage your personal development?

6) How is chanting similar to and different from conventional Western concepts of prayer? The authors claim you need not even believe in chanting for it to work. Can you accept this without questioning its validity or demanding proof? If you've tried to chant, discuss your experience.

7) The authors claim, "All of us are ultimately responsible for everything about our lives." (Page 79) When you look back at some painful or hurtful events in your life, can you accept 100% responsibility as Buddhism asks?

8) According to Buddhism, there are no accidents in life and there are no coincidences (page 83). How does knowing this change how you view situations that surface in your life? Is there something that has recently happened that puzzles you?

9) In the Buddhist view, our lives are like pages in a book. Our eternal lives extend beyond our physical lives. Is this view very different from other faith perspectives on life after life on earth?

CARAMELO

Author: Sandra Cisneros

Publisher: Knopf, 2002

Website: www.aaknopf.com

Available in:
Hardcover, 448 pages, $24.00
(ISBN: 0-679-43554-9)
Also in a Spanish-language edition

Genre: Fiction/
Hispanic Culture/Family Issues

Summary

Lala Reyes's grandmother is descended from a family of renowned shawl makers—the striped (or caramelo) being the most beautiful of all, and the one that makes its way, like the family history it has come to represent, into Lala's possession. The novel opens with the Reyes's annual car trip—a child-filled, laughter-filled, quarrel-filled caravan—from Chicago to "the other side": Mexico City, where Lala hears her family's stories, separating the truth from the "healthy lies" that have ricocheted from one generation to the next. We travel from Mexico City to Chicago at the dawn of the Roaring Twenties—and to Lala's own difficult childhood in the not-quite-promised land of San Antonio, Texas. This multigenerational story bridges Mexican, Mexican-American, and American cultures.

Recommended by: Dorothy Allison, author of *Bastard Out of Carolina*

"In Caramelo, Sandra Cisneros sings to my blood. Her words are sweet and filling, not sugar-driven but as substantial as meat on the bone. Hers is the kind of family I know well ... she has done them justice on the page; she has given them to us whole."

Author Biography

Sandra Cisneros, born in Chicago in 1954, has been the recipient of numerous awards, including the Lannan Literary Award and the American Book Award, and fellowships from the National Endowment for the Arts and the MacArthur Foundation. She lives in the Southwest.

Topics to Consider

1) From the novel's opening epigraph—"Tell me a story, even it it's a lie."—to its end, the relationship between truth, lies, history, and storytelling is an important theme. Is the reader to believe that Caramelo is just a "different kind of lie" (p. 250)?

2) Celaya says, "I'm not ashamed of my past. It's the story of my life I'm sorry about." (p. 410). What's the difference?

3) What exactly is the nature or power of the "destiny" that the characters seem to revere? Who or what is really in control of the lives and histories portrayed? How is destiny different for Celaya, her grandmother, her parents, and her friend Viva?

4) What aspects, if any, of the Awful Grandmother's life story parallel Celaya's life story? Are the Awful Grandmother and Celaya alike in character, and if so, in what ways? What does the Awful Grandmother teach Celaya about herself?

5) What is the role played in the novel by the various Mexican or Mexican-American figures of popular culture who have encounters with members of the Reyes family? How does Cisneros use these characters to convey both the individuality as well as the universality of the Mexican-American immigrant experience?

6) The characters in Caramelo make frequent observations about Mexicans. Do people of other cultures make similarly deprecating comments, and what purpose might making such comments serve for such people?

7) How does Caramelo reflect the immigrant experience generally for the middle part of the twentieth century, and how have changes within the United States both socially and politically affected the contemporary immigrant experience?

8) Cisneros employs elaborate and vivid food metaphors, such as "Regina was like the papaya slices she sold with lemon and a dash of chile; you could not help but want to take a little taste." (p. 121) Is taste the strongest sense her metaphors invoke? How does she also invoke the senses of smell, sight, and sound? What does Cisneros achieve stylistically or thematically by invoking these senses?

For more discussion topics, see www.randomhouse.com/knopf

DESIRABLE DAUGHTERS

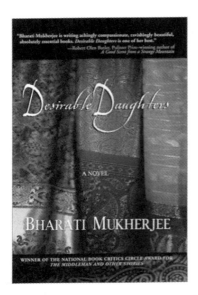

Author: Bharati Mukherjee

Publisher: Hyperion, 2002

Website: www.HyperionBooks.com

Available in:
Hardcover, 320 pages, $24.95
(ISBN 0-7868-6598-9)
Paperback (3/03), 320 pages, $13.95
(ISBN 0-7868-8515-7)

Genre: Fiction/International/
Multicultural/Coming of age

Summary

Desirable Daughters follows the diverging paths taken by three Calcutta-born sisters as they come of age in a changing world. Tara, Padma, and Parvati were born into a wealthy Brahmin family presided over by their doting father and his traditionalist mother. Intelligent and artistic, the girls are nevertheless constrained by a society with little regard for women. Their subsequent rebellion will lead them in different directions, to different continents, and through different circumstances that strain yet ultimately strengthen their relationship.

Recommended by: *New York Times*

"Her most thoughtful, emotionally detailed book yet."

Author Biography

Bharati Mukherjee is the author of five novels, two nonfiction books, and a collection of short stories, *The Middleman and Other Stories*, for which she won the National Book Critics Circle Award. She is currently a professor at the University of California at Berkeley.

Topics to Consider

1) What does the title mean, and who are the Desirable Daughters in this story?

2) What do you learn about Tara and her family through the ancient story of Tara Lata Gangooly?

3) Examine what Tara means when she says she is "exploring the making of a consciousness ... No. Yours." (page 5) Discuss whether or not this is a central theme of the book, and why.

4) When do you begin to doubt "Chris Dey's" story and why is Tara dismissive of her sister Parvati's take on it?

5) Why is Andy so off base about Chris Dey and Bish more responsive?

6) Explore why Didi, who as a child eschewed her family and culture, leads a traditional Bengali life in New Jersey?

7) On page 33, look at the paragraph beginning "Bengali culture ..." Discuss the idea that the narrator is also describing an essential dilemma of cultures.

8) Look at the Tennyson poem on page 132. What does it mean—on its own and in the story?

9) Why are there so many houses prominently featured throughout the story, and what is symbolic about Tara's home being destroyed?

10) Why does Tara say to Rabi, "remember, this is a miracle?" (page 310)

THE ELEGANT GATHERING OF WHITE SNOWS

Author: Kris Radish

Publisher: Spinsters Ink, 2002

Website: www.spinsters-ink.com

Available in:
Paperback, 335 pages, $14.00
(ISBN 1-883523-42-7)

Genre: Fiction/
Friendship/Women's Issues

Summary

While meeting ostensibly as a Bible study group for several years, a group of Southeastern Wisconsin farm women have become close friends. Like all women, they have shared a deep secret, a heartache, a loss, an emotional pain that has kept each one of them from moving forward. When one woman confesses that she has just discovered that she is pregnant and what the baby is not her husband's, the confession pushes them to a place of action. That action starts with a journey that begins in the middle of the night. Grabbing coats and shoes, they head out for a walk with no end. Using the passion and love that has bonded them together and a bit of wine, each one of the women during this walk reaches a decision that turns into a life-altering expression of personal growth and forgiveness.

Recommended by: Kate Bast, *Wisconsin Trails Magazine*

"Inquisitive, sensitive and attuned to details, Kris Radish has all the hallmarks of a great writer."

Author Biography

Kris Radish is a nationally syndicated columnist, author, journalist and Pulitzer Prize finalist. Her liberal political and humor columns appear in newspapers throughout the U.S. and she is the author of the true crime book ***Run, Bambi, Run.*** She has been a working journalist for 25 years, has taught communications courses at two major universities, and has received numerous writing awards.

Topics to Consider

1) Could you identify with the feelings of love and friendship these women walkers have for each other?

2) Has there been a time in your own life when you have wanted to ignore the day-to-day reality of your life and slide out the back door?

3) Which of the eight characters speaks the loudest to you?

4) The issues addressed in this book—depression, abortion, the loss of a child, sacrifice, loneliness, sexual abuse, and abandonment—cross many lines. Was there a particular incident in this book that brought you back to an unanswered place in your own life?

5) There is a powerful call for women to acknowledge the strong bonds they have for each other. How do you feel about that issue?

6) Women always seem to sacrifice their own needs, wants, goals, feelings for everyone else in their lives. In this book, the women walkers carve out a special place for themselves that makes other women call them heroes and some curse them. What is your reaction?

7) The women in this book inspire other women to change and challenge their lives. Who changed and challenged your life? How would you like to give that gift to other women?

8) What can men learn from this book? If you could pick out three important issues for men that are illuminated in this story, what would they be?

9) Whether or not you have a daughter, women want to pass on a legacy of learning and love to their daughters or the daughters of the world that they share. After reading this book, what would you like to say? What would you pass on?

10) What emotions did the telling of this story awaken in you?

11) Has the story of these women walkers inspired you to change or address any issues in your own life that you would love to change?

ELLA MINNOW PEA

Author: Mark Dunn

Publisher: Anchor Books, 2002

Website: www.vintagebooks.com/read

Available in:
Paperback, 224 pages. $12.00
(ISBN 0-385-72243-5)

Genre: Fiction/Language/
Social Commentary

Summary

Ella Minnow Pea is a girl living happily on the fictional island of Nollop off the coast of South Carolina. Nollop was named after Nevin Nollop, author of the immortal pangram, "The quick brown fox jumps over the lazy dog." Now Ella finds herself acting to save her friends, family, and fellow citizens from the encroaching totalitarianism of the island's Council, which has banned the use of certain letters of the alphabet as they fall from a memorial statue of Nevin Nollop. As the letters progressively drop from the statue they also disappear from the novel. The result is both a hilarious and moving story of one girl's fight for freedom of expression, as well as a linguistic tour de force sure to delight word lovers everywhere.

Recommended by: *The Christian Science Monitor*

"There's the whiff of a classic about **Ella Minnow Pea.** *"*

Author Biography

Mark Dunn is the author of more than twenty-five full-length plays, including the widely produced *Belles* and *Five Tellers Dancing in the Rain*. He has received several national playwriting awards and is currently playwright-in-residence with the New Jersey Repertory Company and the Community Theatre League in Williamsport, Pennsylvania. **Ella Minnow Pea** is his first novel.

Topics to Consider

1) How is the story more like a fable than a novel? What characteristics does it share with other fables? Does it offer a clear moral?

2) What does the author gain by eschewing a single narrative voice in favor of many characters writing to one another about the events that beset their island-nation? What ironies are involved in writing letters about the disappearance of the letters of the alphabet?

3) In what sense can **Ella Minnow Pea** be read as a satire of censorship and the restriction of free speech?

4) To avoid being prosecuted by the High Council, all the inhabitants of Nollop are forced to substitute words like "cephalus" for "head" and "sub-terra" for "underground" [p. 99]. What are some of the other more amusing verbal acrobatics they are forced to perform?

5) Nate Warren suggests that Nollop's famous pangram—responsible for his divine status—may have been stolen from someone else. What is Dunn suggesting here about the ways in which human societies venerate and mythologize sacred texts and heroic ancestors?

6) What strategies do the islanders use to protest, oppose, and finally overthrow the tyranny of the High Council? How do these strategies create suspense in the novel?

7) Seen in light of recent events, in the Middle East and elsewhere, can the novel be read as a commentary on religious authoritarianism? What does the novel suggest about the dangers of humans assuming they know God's will with absolute certainty?

8) **Ella Minnow Pea** dwells heavily on the theme of communication—reading, writing, and talking. What is Dunn suggesting by having the members of the High Island Council read the falling letters as signs—supernatural communications from Nollop—which ultimately make communication nearly impossible? What does the novel as whole say about the nature and purpose of communication and community?

For a complete Reading Group Guide,
visit www.vintagebooks.com/read

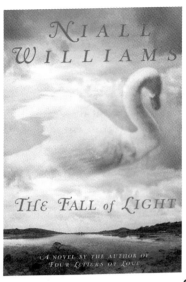

THE FALL OF LIGHT

Author: Niall Williams

Publisher: Warner Books, 2002

Website: www.twbookmark.com

Available in:
Hardcover, 320 pages. $24.95
(ISBN 0-446-52840-4)

Genre: Fiction/Irish Interest/
Immigrant Experience

Summary

Beginning in Ireland in the early years of the 19th century, the four Foley brothers flee across the country with their father and the large telescope he has stolen. Soon forced apart by the violence of the Irish wilderness, the potato famine, and the promise of America, the brothers find themselves scattered across the world. Their separate adventures—which tell the story of Ireland itself—unfold in passionate and vivid scenes with gypsies, horse races, sea voyages, and beautiful women.

Recommended by: *The New York Times Book Review*

"...an unabashed, grandly romantic (and romanticized) saga. ...There is much to relish in Williams's lush and lilting prose."

Author Biography

Niall Williams, author of the critically acclaimed ***Four Letters of Love*** and ***As It Is In Heaven***, delivers a masterful story of one Irish family's remarkable journey to the farthest reaches of the world. He lives in County Clare, Ireland.

Topics to Consider

1) ***The Fall of Light*** purports to be a family legend—a story that has been passed down from generation to generation. Many of the details have changed and will continue to change as the story is told again and again. What is the importance of stories like this? Does your family have a similar story? Does it matter that some of the actual facts of the story get distorted over the years?

2) ***The Fall of Light*** can also be read as an allegory of the Irish people. In what ways do the experiences of the Foley brothers mirror the experience of the Irish people as a whole? Some things to consider: Tomas and Teige's voyage to America; Finan's missionary work in Africa; Finbar's travels around Europe.

3) What is the significance of the stars and the telescope in ***The Fall of Light?*** Why do you think Francis is so fascinated with them?

4) The austere island of Scattery becomes the new home for the Foleys. Is there a similar ancestral home in your family's heritage? Do you think there is any significance in the fact that, like Ireland itself, Scattery is an island? That it is extremely difficult to get to? That it was considered a holy island because of St. Senan's monastery?

5) Francis Foley's single act of rebellion irrevocably changes the course of his family's history. Are there similar events in your own family's history that are responsible for such drastic changes? How are these events considered today?

6) Coincidence appears to play a large role in this novel. Teige finding his mother in Killaloe and coming across Tomas's farm in America are just two examples. Do you think that these meetings are coincidences, or do you believe that these events were fated to happen? Why?

7) Though scattered to the four corners of the world, virtually all of the Foleys yearn to come home again. Why is it that home and family has such a hold on these characters? Why do they have such a hold on us? What compels us to seek home and family out?

8) The relationships between the Foley men and the women in their lives are extremely intense and powerful. What is it about each of these women that generates such feeling? Are there other forces at play which might cause the men to react so strongly to these women?

FALLING ANGELS

Author: Tracy Chevalier

Publisher: Plume Books, 2002

Website: www.tchevalier.com

Available in:
Paperback, 336 pages. $13.00
(ISBN 0-452-28320-5)

Genre: Fiction/History/
Women's Issues

Summary

Time magazine crowned *Girl With a Pearl Earring* "a portrait of radiance...a jewel." In her *New York Times* bestselling follow-up, Tracy Chevalier once again paints a distant age with a rich and provocative palette of characters. Told through a variety of shifting perspectives—wives and husbands, friends and lovers, masters and their servants, and a gravedigger's son—*Falling Angels* follows the fortunes of two families in the emerging years of the twentieth century. Graced with the luminous imagery that distinguished *Girl With a Pearl Earring*, *Falling Angels* is another dazzling tour de force from this "master of voices" (*The New York Times Book Review*).

Recommended by: *The Washington Post Book World*

"Entirely successful: distinct, inhabited, vivid and real."

Author Biography

Tracy Chevalier holds a graduate degree in creative writing from the University of East Anglia. Her novel, *Girl With a Pearl Earring*, has sold over one million copies. An American originally from Washington, D.C., she currently lives in London with her husband and her son.

Topics to Consider

1) Chevalier alternates the narrative point of view to reveal the layered complexities of characters, events, and issues. Which character's perspectives were the most revealing? Which characters do you relate to the most?

2) The turn of the century found England in a state of transition. How did the death of Queen Victoria signify a new era, a more modern climate? How do the conflicting opinions on death and mourning define the characters? In what ways do these differing attitudes indicate the social changes to come?

3) When the Waterhouses and Colemans first meet in the cemetery, what do the characters' first impressions of each other—and of the other family's grave ornament—expose about themselves?

4) How do the issues the female characters face differ with those women are facing now, a century later? What obstacles still exist? How might this story differ if it were set now?

5) The cemetery is a curious place to set a novel. On one hand, it mirrors the outside world, with rigid rules of conduct that mourners are expected to follow. On the other hand, both children and adults experience a degree of freedom there. How does the making and breaking of rules there reflect on and affect the characters?

6) Lavinia, Simon, and Maude appear to represent the past, present, and future respectively. Does this change at all throughout the novel? What do they learn from each other?

7) What is Ivy May Waterhouse's role in the book? Why does she meet such a fate?

8) They say an Englishman's home is his castle. How do Kitty's and Gertrude's houses reflect their characters and class differences?

Additional topics for discussion can be found at:
www.penguinputnam.com/guides

FAMILY MATTERS

Author: Rohinton Mistry

Publisher: Knopf, 2002

Website: www.aaknopf.com

Available in:
Hardcover, 448 pages, $26.00
(ISBN: 0-375-40373-6)

Genre: Fiction/Family Issues/
Indian Culture

Summary

The setting is Bombay, mid-1990s. Nariman Vakeel, suffering from Parkinson's disease, is the elderly patriarch of a small, discordant family. He and his two middle-aged stepchildren—Coomy, bitter and domineering, and her brother, Jal, mild mannered and acquiescent—occupy a once-elegant apartment whose ruin progresses as rapidly as Nariman's disease. When his illness is compounded by a broken ankle, Coomy plots to turn his round-the-clock care over to her younger, sweet-tempered half sister—living with her husband and two sons in an already overcrowded apartment—knowing that Roxana will not refuse. What ensues is a great unraveling, and repair, of the family, and a revelation of its love-torn past.

Recommended by: *The Saturday Post*

"Once again Rohinton Mistry has written an absolutely fabulous novel...one of the best writers working in the English language today."

Author Biography

Rohinton Mistry was born in Bombay and now lives near Toronto. His first novel, **Such a Long Journey**, received, among other awards, the 1992 Commonwealth Writers Prize for Best Book of the Year. In 1995, **A Fine Balance** won the second annual Giller Prize and the *Los Angeles Times* Book Prize for Fiction.

Topics to Consider

1) Why did Nariman give in, after his eleven-year love affair with Lucy, to his parents' demand that he marry a Parsi woman? He was forty-two years old at the time. Was his decision an act of weakness?

2) What is the novel's perspective on the state of India's politics, compared with the idealism of Mahatma Gandhi? Is Nariman a cynic, a wit, or simply a realist at this stage of his experience?

3) Most of the novel's events take place in two apartments. What perspective do the names of these buildings—Chateau Felicity and Pleasant Villas—cast on the lives lived within them? Why is it important to our comprehension of Bombay life that we understand just how little space people are living in?

4) Why does Mistry suggest, as in his Tolstoyan epigraph, that "all unhappy families resemble one another"? To what degree does family unhappiness result from constant togetherness?

5) Does Coomy force the care of Nariman onto Roxana as an act of revenge? Is it understandable that, given her loyalty to her mother's memory, Coomy would resent having to tend her ailing stepfather? Why are the circumstances of Coomy's death particularly ironic?

6) Several characters take steps to alleviate their difficulties; strenuous efforts to arrange the events of their lives come to grief. Does Mistry suggest that fate—rather than desire or will—rules human lives?

7) Of all the characters in the story, Roxana is the one who understands most fully the weighty responsibilities that come with loving one's family. How does this understanding impinge upon her happiness? Is she too self-sacrificing?

8) How do realizations about loving service, as well as the awareness of mortality, affect the ethical thinking of Mistry's characters?

9) The novel's epilogue is presented by Jehangir, now fourteen. Why has Mistry chosen to make Jehangir a central consciousness in the novel? What are we to make of Jehangir's final words?

For additional topics, see www.randomhouse.com/knopf

FOR THE SAKE OF PEACE
Seven Paths to Global Harmony

Author: Daisaku Ikeda

Publisher: Middleway Press, 2002

Website: www.middlewaypress.org

Available in:
Paperback, 252 pages. $14.00
(ISBN 0-9674697-9-1)

Genre: Nonfiction/Social Issues

Summary

The lives of people everywhere were touched by the events in the United States on September 11. Although war, hate, hunger, and terrorism are hardly new to the world, there has been a renewed interest in what it might take to achieve peace across the globe. If you've ever wondered how such a lofty goal could be attained, and how one can make a difference, this book, winner of NAPRA's Nautilus Award in the Social Change category, offers insights, information and wisdom to give readers hope that things can be better.

Drawn from the author's 25+ years of university work and involvement with the United Nations, *For the Sake of Peace* addresses the issue of peace from the perspectives of compassion, the interconnectedness of all life and the absolute respect for human life—principles of Buddhist thought. With an understanding of the mistakes of the past, a clear picture of the emotions and issues that have evolved, and a compassionate message about the possibilities for the future, Dr. Ikeda offers us seven paths to peace—from self-mastery and dialogue to global awareness and disarmament—that will help us overcome major obstacles to the well-being of people everywhere.

Author Biography

Daisaku Ikeda is the founder of numerous cultural and educational institutes throughout the world. He has written more than 200 books that have been translated into several languages, and has worked tirelessly for international cultural exchange and the establishment of world peace.

Topics to Consider

1) Have people you've known experienced war first-hand? Were they able to share what they experienced? Although difficult for most to tell and to hear, discuss the importance of those stories to a society.

2) Since the end of the Cold War in 1989, a time when many felt hopeful for the future, more than fifty nations have been in violent conflicts and millions of lives have been claimed. What were your thoughts about the prospects for world peace at that time? Did they change after September 11? Have those thoughts changed after reading this book?

3) Dialogue is one of the critical steps toward peace, according to Dr. Ikeda. Is there ever a case where dialogue should be halted as a peace-keeping strategy?

4) How might your upbringing have influenced the kind of dialogue with which you feel most comfortable—or, most threatened?

5) Do you agree with the theory that "a borderless economy results in homogenization and a standardized consumer culture?" (p. 78) Is it possible for countries to open their borders to corporations with a global "brand" and still retain their identity? Discuss what you've observed about the strength of cultural identity during your travels to different countries.

6) If, as the author suggests, "the United States represents global society in miniature and foreshadows, for better or worse, the humanity of tomorrow (p. 80)," what changes in the U.S. can help the world achieve harmony?

7) Dr. Ikeda stresses that "We must resist the temptation to assign good exclusively to one side and evil to the other." (p. 115) What role does the news media play in polarizing issues—and people?

8) Many suggest that politicians create war and that if it were up to the people, we would avoid violent conflicts. What evidence supports this belief? What evidence disputes it? What is your personal belief?

9) Review and discuss the preamble of the World Citizens Charter that is presented on page 179. Do you believe the people of the world can have the patience and fortitude needed? If it is up to the people to create lasting change, what steps can you take to be a part of this global effort?

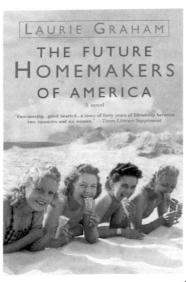

FUTURE HOMEMAKERS OF AMERICA

Author: Laurie Graham

Publisher: Warner, 2002

Website: www.twbookmark.com

Available in:
Paperback, 432 pages. $14.00
(ISBN 0-446-67936-4)

Genre: Fiction/Women's Issues/
Friendship/Home Life

Summary

In the tradition of **Divine Secrets of the Ya-Ya Sisterhood**, this moving novel is about a group of women who discover—over the course of 40 turbulent years—the nature of true friendship. Stationed at a U.S. Air Force base in Norfolk, England in 1952, a group of "Yankee wives" are thrown together by nothing more than husbands who patrol the skies keeping the Soviets at bay. They seem to have little in common; some, like Pie Crust Queen Betty Gillis, are content to clip coupons and bake chocolate brownies, while others, like good-time girl Lois Moon, look for a little excitement beyond the perimeter fence. But the women soon discover similarities, from a common fear for their husbands to a desire to help out the war-ravaged British natives. Through marriage and divorce, separations and reunions, the gang will try to hold fast to each other in a story that takes us to the heart of female friendship—and reveals the secret of the perfect Three Color Refrigerator Cake.

Recommended by: *Times Literary Supplement (UK)*

"Fast-moving...good-hearted...a story of forty years of friendship between two countries and six women."

Author Biography

Laurie Graham is a former *Daily Telegram* columnist and Contributing Editor to *Cosmopolitan UK*. This is her sixth novel, and she is currently writing the screenplay adaptation for her novel *The Dress Circle*.

Topics to Consider

1) What role does the "homemaker" play in the book? What does homemaker mean to you? How would you or someone you know who is a homemaker relate to the homemakers in this book? Has the concept/role of a homemaker changed dramatically since the 1950s and 1960s, and if so, how? Do you think a career woman of today can also be a homemaker?

2) Why do you think the author decided to begin her book with a historical event, the death of King George VI? What sort of impact does this news have on the wives? What parallels, if any, do you see between this event in history and the point in these women's lives?

3) Do you see differences between the Englishwoman Kath Pharaoh and the American ladies? Are there any instances of culture clash, despite their friendship? Have you ever experienced culture clash? If so, discuss your experience.

4) Do you believe that life as the wife of an officer on a base has changed over the decades? What are the advantages and disadvantages of being an officer's wife on a military base? What sort of community does this provide? How does life in this type of community compare to other types of communities?

5) The author includes character-specific recipes throughout the novel. What do they say about the individual characters? What do your favorite recipes say about you? Did you try any of these recipes at home?

6) Do you think the historical references included in the novel add texture, or did you find them distracting? How do these historical events affect these characters? What events in history have dramatically affected your life?

THE GOSPEL OF JUDAS

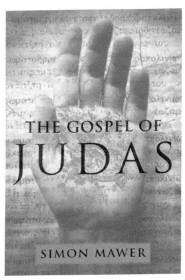

Author: Simon Mawer

Publisher: Little, Brown & Co., 2002

Website: www.twbookmark.com

Available in:
Paperback, 352 pages. $13.95
(ISBN 0-316-97374-2)

Genre: Fiction/History/
Suspense/Faith & Religion

Summary

A priest experiencing a crisis of faith—and the married woman to whom he is attracted. A scroll newly discovered near Jerusalem that, if authentic, could open Christianity to a complete reinterpretation. A tragic love affair unfolding in Fascist-dominated Rome during World War II. These are the elements of a magnificent literary entertainment—a novel that resonates with tales of love and betrayal as it deals profoundly with questions of faith and what it means to believe.

Recommended by: *The Boston Globe*

"A superior novel....A noteworthy achievement....An intellectual thriller of uncommon substance."

Author Biography

Simon Mawer has written about Italy directly in ***A Place in Italy,*** published in UK in 1992, and set two of his other novels partly in the country—***Chimera*** (1989), and now ***The Gospel of Judas.*** He is a biologist by training; it was with the biology of genetics that his last novel ***Mendel's Dwarf*** dealt. Mawer has lived in Italy for over two decades, and is married with a son and a daughter.

Topics to Consider

1) Which character in **The Gospel of Judas** did you most closely identify with? Explain why.

2) There are three important female characters in the novel—Madaleine; Magda; and Leo's mother, Gretchen. What role does each woman play in Leo's life? How does each woman's life experience contribute to Leo's understanding of the world and his own place in it?

3) What did you think was the most surprising moment in the novel? Why?

4) Have you had a pivotal moment in your own life that made you re-evaluate everything that came before?

5) What do you think is at stake if Father Leo Newman validates the scroll? And if he denies its authenticity?

6) What do you imagine is the significance of Leo Newman's name? In what way does Leo's character change in the course of the novel?

7) There are three storylines running through the novel. In what ways do they overlap, intersect, resonate? How did the novel's structure influence your reading of the book and your enjoyment of it?

8) **The Gospel of Judas** has been described as a novel of betrayal and resurrection. Can you trace these themes through the narrative? Do you think Leo's resurrection in the present-day passages is a triumph or a failure?

9) Discuss the contrast between the Italy of Leo's youth and the Italy of his adulthood.

10) Does **The Gospel of Judas** remind you of any other literary thrillers you've read? How are the books similar? How are they different?

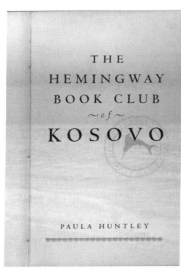

THE HEMINGWAY BOOK CLUB OF KOSOVO

Author: Paula Huntley

Publisher: Tarcher/Putnam, 2/2003

Website: www.penguinputnam.com

Available in:
Hardcover, 271 pages. $22.95
(ISBN 1-58542-211-8)

Genre: Nonfiction/Memoir/
Travel/Multicultural

Summary

Kosovo, 2000. After a decade of brutal civil war and apartheid, volunteers had arrived from all over the world to help. When her husband signed on to help rebuild Kosovo's legal system, Paula Huntley agreed to accompany him for a year. Wanting to make herself useful in some way, Huntley found a job teaching English to a group of Kosovo Albanians in the city of Prishtina. Then, one day, she found an English-language copy of Hemingway's *The Old Man and the Sea* in a bookstore, and an American-style book club was born. This is the diary of Huntley's book club and her other unforgettable experiences in Kosovo.

Recommended by: Mary Pipher, author of *Reviving Ophelia*

"Huntley is an excellent storyteller. This book is filled with heart and intelligence, which is my definition of wisdom."

Author Biography

Paula Huntley was reluctant to give up the familiarity of her life in Northern California, but did so to support her husband Ed's desire to somehow make a difference in Kosovo. Having at one time taught history, she took a course in Teaching English as a Second Language, and brought her personal experience with a book group to her new students.

If you would like to learn about ways to help young Kosovars receive a good education or about other ways to help the people of Kosovo, please e-mail the author directly at bookclubofkosovo@yahoo.com.

Topics to Consider

1) Huntley tries to teach her students about the perils of stereotyping to avoid saying, "All Americans are this, all Serbs are that," and so forth. Do you ever find yourself stereotyping? Why is it so easy or appealing to stereotype?

2) Discuss the notion of collective guilt and collective innocence. Do you feel that the Albanians who unequivocally hate Serbs are justified in their hatred? Do you feel that they can, and should, overcome their hatred for the sake of rebuilding their country?

3) If your country were at war, and someone from the other side burned down your house or killed members of your family, would you be able to overcome your feelings about that person and about his/her people for the sake of moving on?

4) Leonard, the Professor, and Huntley's other students demonstrated incredible hope and optimism despite terrible adversity. What in their lives or in their personalities made this possible? Can you imagine yourself, under the same circumstances, demonstrating such hope and optimism?

5) Although there has been progress, Albanian women are at times treated as second-class citizens. How can the U.S. and other countries help modernize or democratize Kosovo while respecting their history and differences from other western countries? Or should we be insisting on 100 percent equal rights for women in exchange for our aid?

6) Do you think that journals, in general, translate into good books? Did you like the fact that **The Hemingway Book Club of Kosovo** was never intended to be a book, and is in fact a series of spontaneous, uncensored journal entries by an ordinary woman, i.e. not a journalist or historian? Do you keep a journal? Can you imagine turning it into a book? When does something that is meaningful to you personally become something that might be meaningful for a wider audience?

7) Have you ever fantasized about dropping everything, seeing the world, and also doing volunteer work in another country? Where do you imagine going? What kind of volunteer work do you imagine doing?

8) Are there lessons we can take from this book personally, spiritually, politically, and otherwise that can help us deal with the turmoil of our post-September-11 world?

THE IMPRESSIONIST

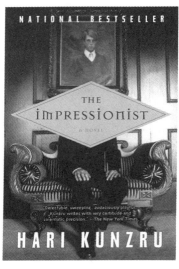

Author: Hari Kunzru

Publisher: Plume, 2003

Website: www.harikunzru.com

Available in:
Paperback, 400 pages, $14.00
(ISBN 0-452-28397-3)

Genre: Fiction/Multicultural/
Indian Culture

Summary

Fathered, through circuitous circumstances, by an Englishman, Pran Nath Razdan, the boy who will become the Impressionist, was passed off by his Indian mother as the child of her husband, a wealthy man of high caste. At fifteen, the news of Pran's true parentage is revealed to his father and he is tossed out into the street—a pariah and an outcast. Thus begins an extraordinary journey of a young man who must reinvent himself to survive—not once, but many times. From Victorian India to Edwardian London, from an expatriate community of black Americans in Paris to a hopeless expedition to study a lost tribe of Africa, this novel challenges with its insights into what it means to be Indian or English, black or white, and every degree that lies between them.

Recommended by: *The New York Times*

"A sprawling, ambitious, shape-shifting novel ... Kunzru proves himself a clever, sharply observant writer."

Author Biography

Born in London and raised in Essex, **Hari Kunzru** is a freelance journalist and editor living in London. He has written for a variety of English and international publications, including *The Guardian, Daily Telegraph, The Economist,* and *Wired* and was named "Young Travel Writer of the Year" by the *Observer* in 1999. This is his first novel.

Topics to Consider

1) Does the protagonist choose to adopt each new guise, or do pressures of the political or social climate force him to find a new persona? When does he exhibit free will in his decision to change?

2) In every manifestation, the title character must face caste systems and social hierarchies. Discuss the various make-up of the societies and the working of their social construct. Does he ever penetrate one of these sects or is he perpetually an outsider?

3) Discuss the concept of pure blood versus mixed. How did the British imperialistic campaign, the Great War for Civilisation, contribute to the extreme opinions regarding race and culture?

4) The tiger hunt exposed countless political and personal motivations. How was the Nawab's party attempting to indulge the visiting British faction? What other schemes were devised to earn the loyalty of the English?

5) The duplicity of the Impressionist's skin could not create alternate identities on its own. Discuss the various attire worn by the Impressionist in his many incarnations. From schoolboy uniforms and silk saris to academic robes and adventurer's khakis, how did his clothing shape others' impressions?

6) After assuming the role of Jonathan Bridgeman, the main character had only one fearful brush with exposure. How does he deal with his meeting with Aunt Berthilda? What conclusions regarding perception can be drawn from the Headmaster's and Mr. Spavin's reactions to the event?

7) When he is dispelled from his home, Pran considers himself entirely Indian. At what point, and under what influences, does he begin to recognize his English heritage. Why does he not strive harder to re-establish himself as an Indian?

8) In the end, what connections can be drawn between the Impressionist and his biological parents? What has he inherited from them?

Additional topics for discussion can be found at:
www.penguinputnam.com/guides

IN PATERSON

Author: Miriam Levine

Publisher: Southern Methodist
University Press, 2002

Website: hometown.aol.com/
miriamlevine39/inpatersonanovel.html

Available in:
Hardcover, 265 pages. $22.50
(ISBN 0-87074-467-4)

Genre: Fiction/Family/Americana

Summary

    This novel is loosely based on a newspaper account of a
New Jersey domestic tragedy. The protagonist, European-born widower
Ben Shein, is middle-aged, a successful furrier in Paterson, New Jersey, in
the early 1940s. Lonely and ghost-haunted by his dead wife Tess, Ben pursues and marries the young and beautiful shopgirl Judith Karger against the
advice of his brother Nat, who struggles to leave the family's fur business.
Their marriage soon disintegrates, and Ben's ten-year-old daughter Susan
becomes an innocent victim of the bitter unhappiness between her father
and stepmother. Paterson is as much a character as any of the city's inhabitants and comes to stand for any urban American locale where immigrants
strive to assimilate as they play out the dramas of their lives.

Recommended by: Julia Markus

*"Riveting. Levine recreates a family tragedy with the surety of stroke of a Goya, a Rem-
brandt, bringing the reader from the deep, shadow side of human nature to the filtered
light of redemption. I couldn't put this book down."*

Author Biography

    Born in Paterson, New Jersey, **Miriam Levine** is the author of ***Devo-
tion: A Memoir***, three poetry collections, and ***A Guide to Writers'
Homes in New England***. Levine chairs the English Department at
Framingham State College near Boston and divides her time between
Massachusetts and Miami Beach, Florida. Currently she's at work on a new
novel and a poetry collection.

Topics to Consider

1) What role does the desire for love play in the lives of the major characters?

2) Discuss the dreams Ben Shein has of his dead wife Tess. What did Tess mean to him and to their surviving daughter Susan?

3) Why does Ben Shein want to marry again? Why does he choose Judith Karger against the warnings of his brother Nat?

4) Compare the relationships of the various paired characters: the lovers, Judith and Ben, Renee and Nat; the friends, Susan and Joan; the parent, Brona with each of her sons. What other pairs do you find?

5) What emotions do you feel for the stepmother Judith Karger?

6) Discuss the life and career of the furrier Ben Shein, tremendously successful in business, tragically flawed in his search for love.

7) How is the Shein family shaped by their immigrant experience? Can the Sheins maintain their ethnic identity and at the same time assimilate into American society?

8) In what ways does the author avoid stereotyped portrayals of Jews? How do the various characters, many from different backgrounds, interact with each other?

9) What role does Joe Mavet play in the novel?

10) Discuss the transmuting of newspaper headlines into fiction. How do the events of this novel relate to today's news stories of passion and violence in families? Is it possible to really explain the forces that drive people to desperate acts?

JENNY

Author: Sigrid Undset

Translator: Tiina Nunnally

Publisher: Steerforth Press, 2002

Website: www.steerforth.com

Available in:
Paperback, 310 pages. $16.00
(ISBN 1-58642-050-X)

Genre: Fiction/Women's Issues/Art

Summary

When **Jenny** was published in 1911, Undset found herself called immoral—"this is a side of the free, artistic life that the vast majority of citizens would rather not know." The novel tells the story of Jenny Winge, a talented Norwegian painter who goes to Rome to seek artistic inspiration but ultimately betrays her own ambitions and ideals. Undset's portrayal of a woman struggling toward independence and fulfillment is written with an unflinching, clear-eyed honesty that renders her story as compelling today as it was nearly a century ago.

Recommended by: *Booklist*

*'**Jenny** is a stunningly atmospheric yet frank and searching drama about a young woman painter struggling to reconcile her need to make art with her longing for and fear of love. This brooding book can stand with the best of the moderns."*

Author Biography

Sigrid Undset won the Nobel Prize for Literature in 1928. Her early novels portrayed modern women "sympathetically but with merciless truthfulness"; her later works, including the internationally bestselling Kristin Lavransdatter trilogy, contained "powerful pictures of Northern life in medieval times."

Tiina Nunnaly won the 2001 PEN/Book-of-the-Month Club Translation Prize for her translation of the Penguin Classics *Kristin Lavransdatter* trilogy. She lives in Seattle.

Topics to Consider

1) When *Jenny* was first published in 1911, Sigrid Undset was called immoral—"this is a side of the free, artistic life that the vast majority of citizens would rather not know." What would critics say today about a novel with the same story line, written in contemporary western culture?

2) Compare the social and family expectations of young women today to the young women who lived in Jenny's era.

3) While Jenny was presented as responsible and independent for much of the novel, in the end her humanness cannot be contained. What aspects of Jenny's life helped form her character? What aspects drove her to such a tragic end?

4) Explore the nature of Jenny's friendship with Fransiska. What did each receive from the friendship? What did each give? Would you have considered Cesca a true friend?

5) Discuss the challenges Jenny faced in her relationships with Helga, Gert, and Gunnar and her attempt to hold onto her old moral view, which was essentially based on truthfulness and restraint (Page 83).

6) Was Jenny justified in withholding truth from her mother? What were the spoken and unspoken reasons for Jenny doing so? How would you imagine Jenny's mother felt upon learning the news of her daughter's death?

7) Why did Jenny get involved with Gert Gramm? How did she benefit from the relationship? What did Gert need from Jenny?

8) Discuss the experience of marriage in this novel and how duty, power, betrayal, and secrets shaped the marriages between Gert and Rebekka and Cesca and Lennart. What was Undset's statement to her contemporaries about the pursuit of love and marriage and the role of women in this relationship?

9) Discuss Gunnar's personal journey in the book. What was Undset's reason for writing him into the story?

10) What did Undset reveal about life for women during the early 1900s that made her novel so controversial? Was the tragic ending of the novel necessary to invoke such a response? Although the novel was written long ago, how is the story still relevant today?

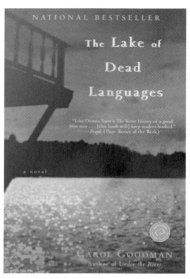

THE LAKE OF DEAD LANGUAGES

Author: Carol Goodman

Publisher: Ballantine Books, 1/2003

Website:
www.ballantinebooks.com/BRC

Available in:
Paperback, 416 pages. $13.95
(ISBN 0-345-45089-2)

Genre: Fiction/Mystery/
Young Adult Issues

Summary

Twenty years ago, Jane Hudson left the Heart Lake School for Girls in the Adirondacks after a terrible tragedy. Now she has returned as a Latin teacher, recently separated and hoping to make a fresh start with her young daughter. Since freshmen year, Jane and her two roommates, Lucy Toller and Deirdre Hall, were inseparable. However, the last winter before graduation, everything changed. Three lives were taken, all victims of senseless suicide. Only Jane was left to carry the burden of a mystery that has stayed hidden for more than two decades in the dark depths of Heart Lake. Now pages from Jane's missing journal, written during that tragic time, have reappeared, revealing shocking, long-buried secrets. And suddenly, young, troubled girls are beginning to die again ... as piece by piece the shattering truth slowly floats to the surface.

Recommended by: *The Cleveland Plain-Dealer*

"Emotionally gripping ... Peppered with powerful truths."

Author Biography

Carol Goodman's work has appeared in such journals as *The Greensboro Review*, *Literal Latté*, *The Midwest Quarterly*, and *Other Voices*. After graduating from Vassar College, she taught Latin for several years in Austin, Texas. She then received an M.F.A. in fiction from the New School University. Goodman currently teaches writing and works as a writer-in-residence for Teachers & Writers. She lives in Long Island.

Topics to Consider

1) Given the trauma she endured there, why does Jane return to the Heart Lake School for Girls? Do you judge her options to be as limited as she does? Are there other factors at work in her decision?

2) Discuss the nature of Jane and Mitch's marriage and the impact Olivia's birth had on it. How does motherhood change Jane's life?

3) Lucy had a magnetism that drew people to her, inspiring conflict and jealousy within her circle. Have you ever had such a friend or been such a friend?

4) Discuss the particular intensity of adolescent friendships and the havoc they can wreak as well as the benefits.

5) Discuss the many secrets finally brought to light in this novel and the corrosive and destructive impact secrets can have on those keeping them and those from whom information is withheld.

6) Jane has lived under a cloud of guilt and remorse since her senior year at Heart Lake. She wonders "if there's any end to this cycle of guilt and retribution." Do you think the truth will set her free?

7) Jane is haunted by a past that has severely compromised her ability to live in the present. Discuss how people can become trapped by the past and how to make peace with it.

8) What shape do you imagine Jane's life will take after the end of this novel? Do you think she will leave Heart Lake? Should she?

9) Choose a character other than Jane and discuss how the story would have unfolded from his or her perspective. What would change and what would remain the same? How would Jane be depicted?

10) If you could invite this author to your book club, what would you like to ask her? What would you want to know about the creation of this novel?

Additional topics for discussion can be found at
www.ballantinebooks.com/BRC

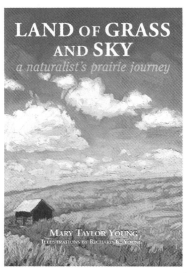

LAND OF GRASS AND SKY
A Naturalist's Prairie Journey

Author: Mary Taylor Young

Publisher: Westcliffe Publishers, 2002

Website: westcliffepublishers.com

Available in:
Paperback, 160 pages. $14.95
(ISBN 1-56579-431-1)

Genre: Nonfiction/Nature/Biography

Summary

Part nature lore, part history, part meditation, this book reveals an intricately-woven landscape of wildlife, plants and people, a place that teaches you to listen with the spirit and see with more than just your eyes. The author's personal story is intertwined with detailed and perceptive tales of the West's open country, from black-tailed prairie dogs and nighthawks to chokecherries and buffalo grass. Young examines the human impact on the prairie from the Dust Bowl years to today which is especially timely in light of the recent drought and explosion of wildfires in the West. It is the story of the author's journey from the ending of a marriage to a new love, from dependence to self-reliance, and how she learned to see the beauties of a subtle landscape, and of herself.

Recommended by: Ann Zwinger, author of *Beyond the Aspen Grove*

"[This] charming love letter to the prairies and grasslands shows once again that the natural world provides unlimited inspiration for a quick observer and graceful writer."

Author Biography

Mary Taylor Young is a professional naturalist, author of nine books including **The Guide To Colorado Birds** and **On The Trail Of Colorado Critters**, and columnist for the *Rocky Mountain News*. Mary's work has appeared in the magazines *Outside, Ladies Home Journal, Birder's World,* and numerous other publications. She is a former board member of the Audubon Society of Greater Denver and teaches summer nature writing workshops at Rocky Mountain National Park.

Topics to Consider

1) In the introduction, the author describes a family road trip. Does this bring back similar memories from childhood for you? Have you ever traveled across the Great Plains and what was your reaction? Might you reconsider that viewpoint after having read the book?

2) The author concludes the introduction by saying that while she traveled by foot, car and horseback, her journey was one of the spirit. What did she mean? What was the author's journey?

3) The author said she learned to see with more than her eyes and to listen to silence to discover the fullness of an empty land. What does that mean and how do you do that? How does her growing love of this subtle landscape apply to appreciating other people and ourselves?

4) What does the book tell us about the plants and animals of the prairie, how they are adapted to that habitat, and their interrelationships? What native plant and animal species form the cornerstone for the natural communities in your region?

5) 2002 was a year of severe drought and wildfires in the West, particularly in the region of Colorado covered by this book. What does the author tell us about these phenomena, their causes and how they fit into natural cycles? What are the environmental lessons of the book?

6) What rivers and streams are in your area? How did they affect the way the land is formed, what plants grow where, and the human history of your area?

7) The author followed rivers from her home at the foot of the Rocky Mountains to where? What personal connections did she discover and what conclusion did it bring her to about her own life?

8) The author visits a rancher who grew up in a sod house. Consider your own family history and heritage and think about ways past generations of your family were connected to the land. Contrast your childhood or that of your parents with Gene Vick's upbringing on the Colorado prairie. How would you be different today if you had grown up in such circumstances?

9) After reading the book, in what ways did you come to appreciate the prairie? What other things might it have triggered an interest in?

LONG DAY'S JOURNEY INTO NIGHT

Author: Eugene O'Neill

Publisher: Yale University Press, 2002

Website: www.yalebooks.com

Available in:
Paperback, 180 pages, $12.95
(ISBN 0-300-09305-5)

Genre: Fiction/Drama

Summary

Eugene O'Neill's autobiographical play is regarded as his finest work. First published in 1956, it won the Pulitzer Prize in 1957 and has since sold more than one million copies. This edition includes a new foreword by Harold Bloom, who writes: "The helplessness of family love to sustain, let alone heal, the wounds of marriage, of parenthood, and of sonship, have never been so remorselessly and so pathetically portrayed, and with a force of gesture too painful ever to be forgotten by any of us."

Recommended by: José Quintero

"Only an artist of O'Neill's extraordinary skill and perception can draw the curtain on the secrets of his own family to make you peer into your own. [This play] is the most remarkable achievement of one of the world's greatest dramatists."

Author Biography

Eugene O'Neill (1888-1953), the father of American drama, began writing plays in 1913, and by 1916 his one-act play *Bound East for Cardiff* was produced in New York. In 1920 his full-length play *Beyond the Horizon* was produced and won O'Neill the first of his four Pulitzer Prizes. Over the next few decades, O'Neill published 24 other full-length plays. After receiving the Nobel Prize for literature in 1936, he published two of his most highly acclaimed plays, *The Iceman Cometh* and *A Moon for the Misbegotten*. *Long Day's Journey Into Night* was published three years after his death.

Topics to Consider

1) Discuss O'Neill's use of stage directions. How does the language employed by O'Neill in his directions differ from that spoken by the characters? How do these directions serve to deepen our understanding of action and characters?

2) How does O'Neill conceive of the possibilities of American life? Marriage? Parenthood?

3) How do dreams function to deepen our understanding of the characters? Are any of the characters' dreams attained or attainable?

4) Discuss the issue of substance abuse in the play. What role does it play in the lives of parents and children?

5) Consider the topic of lying. Who lies to whom, when, and for what reasons? Is anyone honest in the play? When?

6) Discuss the subject of monotony — in what the characters do and say, and in the play's setting.

7) Consider the topic of fathers and sons. What kind of relationship does Tyrone have with his two sons? What is the source of the conflict between generations?

LOOK AT ME

Author: Jennifer Egan

Publisher: Anchor Books, 2002

Website: www.vintagebooks.com

Available in:
Paperback, 432 pages, $14.00
(ISBN: 0-385-72135-8)

Genre: Fiction/
Personal Challenges

Summary

A fashion model named Charlotte Swenson emerges from a car accident in her Illinois hometown with her face so badly shattered that it takes eighty titanium screws to reassemble it. She returns to New York still beautiful but oddly unrecognizable, a virtual stranger in the world she once effortlessly occupied. Jennifer Egan threads Charlotte's narrative with those of other casualties of our infatuation with image. There's a deceptively plain teenaged girl embarking on a dangerous secret life, an alcoholic private eye, and an enigmatic stranger who changes names and accents as he prepares an apocalyptic blow against American society. As these narratives inexorably converge, *Look at Me* becomes a mesmerizing intellectual thriller of identity and imposture.

Recommended by: *The New York Times*

"A haunting, sharp, splendidly articulate novel."

Author Biography

Jennifer Egan is the author of the novel ***The Invisible Circus*** (which was released as a movie starring Cameron Diaz and Jordana Brewster), and a collection of stories, ***Emerald City***. Born in Chicago and raised in San Francisco, Egan attended the University of Pennsylvania and St. John's College, Cambridge. Her fiction has appeared in such publications as *The New Yorker*, *Harper's*, *GQ*, and *Ploughshares*, and she is a frequent contributor to *The New York Times Magazine*. She lives in Brooklyn with her husband and son.

Topics to Consider

1) In Charlotte's mind, what does Rockford represent? How is her chosen path a reaction to her place of birth? Is her return to Rockford at the end of the book merely circumstantial, or does it represent a symbolic shift in her perception of her hometown?

2) Why does the concept of "the shadow self" interest Charlotte, and what does that reveal about her character? What do you imagine Charlotte's shadow self looks like? Does it change after her accident?

3) Many of the characters in **Look at Me** undergo major transformations—whether during the course of the novel or before it begins. In what specific ways do the characters change, and how do these changes affect their lives? Which transformations do you find most surprising? How is the idea of transformation linked to the novel's larger thematic concerns about identity and self?

4) While recuperating from her accident and subsequent surgery, Charlotte allows none of her friends or acquaintances to see her. Once people see you in a weakened state, she claims, they'll never forget. Is she right? Is her perspective borne out over the course of the novel, or does it evolve?

5) Misperceptions and misunderstandings play a crucial role in the plot of **Look at Me**—characters often reach for something they believe they see in one another, only to find that they were mistaken, or even purposely deceived. Identify some of these misunderstandings and talk about their significance to the novel as a whole.

6) At the end of the novel, Charlotte demurs, "As for myself, I'd rather not say very much." Indeed, the novel seems intentionally to leave us without a clear sense of what the future holds for its characters. Why do you think Egan has chosen to end her book so ambiguously? What sorts of lives will the Charlottes, Ellen Metcalf/Hauser, Z, Moose, Ricky, and Irene Maitlock go on to live?

For a complete reading group guide, visit
www.vintagebooks.com/read

THE LOVELY BONES

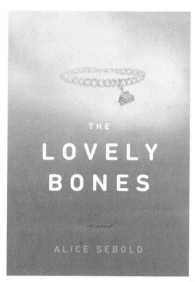

Author: Alice Sebold

Publisher: Little, Brown & Co., 2002

Website: www.twbookmark.com

Available in:
Hardcover, 288 pages. $21.95
(ISBN 0-316-66634-3)

Genre: Fiction/Family Issues

Summary

When we first meet 14-year-old Susie Salmon, she is already in heaven. This was before milk carton photos and public service announcements, she tells us; back in 1973, when Susie mysteriously disappeared, people still believed these things didn't happen. In the sweet, untroubled voice of a precocious teenage girl, Susie relates the awful events of her death, and her own adjustment to the strange new place she finds herself. (It looks a lot like her school playground, with the good kind of swingset.) With love, longing, and a growing understanding, Susie watches her family as they cope with their grief—her father embarks on a search for the killer, her sister undertakes a feat of amazing daring, her little brother builds a fort in her honor—and begin the difficult process of healing.

Recommended by: *The New York Times*

"Ms. Sebold's achievements: her ability to capture both the ordinary and the extraordinary, the banal and the horrific, in lyrical, unsentimental prose; her instinctive understanding of the mathematics of love between parents and children; her gift for making palpable the dreams, regrets and unstilled hopes of one girl and one family."

Author Biography

Alice Sebold is the author of the memoir ***Lucky***. This is her first novel. She lives in Southern California.

Topics to Consider

1) In Susie's Heaven, she is surrounded by things that bring her peace. What would your Heaven be like? Is it surprising that in Susie's inward, personal version of the hereafter there is no God or larger being that presides?

2) Why does Ruth become Susie's main connection to Earth? Was it accidental that Susie touched Ruth on her way up to Heaven, or was Ruth actually chosen to be Susie's emotional conduit?

3) Rape is one of the most alienating experiences imaginable. Susie's rape ends in murder and changes her family and friends forever. Alienation is transferred, in a sense, to Susie's parents and siblings. How do they each experience loneliness and solitude after Susie's death?

4) Why does the author include details about Mr. Harvey's childhood and his memories of his mother? By giving him a human side, does Sebold get us closer to understanding his motivation? Sebold explained in an interview about the novel that murderers "are not animals but men," and that is what makes them so frightening. Do you agree?

5) "Pushing on the inbetween" is how Susie describes her efforts to connect with those she has left behind on Earth. Have you ever felt as though someone was trying to communicate with you from "the inbetween"?

6) Does Buckley really see Susie, or does he make up a version of his sister as a way of understanding, and not being too emotionally damaged by, her death? How do you explain tragedy to a child? Do you think Susie's parents do a good job of helping Buckley comprehend the loss of his sister?

7) In **The Lovely Bones**, adult relationships are dysfunctional and troubled, whereas the young relationships all seem to have depth, maturity, and potential. What is the author saying about young love? About the trials and tribulations of married life?

8) Alice Sebold seems to be saying that out of tragedy comes healing. Susie's family fractures and comes back together, a town learns to find strength in each other. Do you agree that good can come of great trauma?

Additional topics for discussion can be found at www.twbookmark.com.

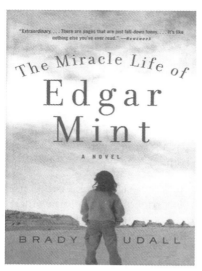

THE MIRACLE LIFE OF EDGAR MINT

Author: Brady Udall

Publisher: Vintage, 2002

Website: www.vintagebooks.com/read

Available in:
Paperback, 432 pages. $14.00
(ISBN 0-375-71918-0)

Genre: Fiction/Language/
Social Commentary

Summary

If I could tell you only one thing about my life it would be this: when I was seven years old the mailman ran over my head. As formative events go, nothing else comes close. With these words Edgar Mint, half-Apache and mostly orphaned, makes his unshakable claim on our attention. In the course of the novel, Edgar survives not just this bizarre accident, but many other experiences which result in the loss of most of the illusions that are supposed to make life bearable. What persists is Edgar's innate goodness, his belief in the redeeming power of language, and his determination to find and forgive the man who almost killed him.

Recommended by: *Newsweek*

"Extraordinary ... Fall-down funny ... It's like nothing else you've ever read."

Author Biography

Brady Udall grew up in a large Mormon family in Arizona, where he worked on his grandfather's farm. He attended the Iowa Writers' Workshop and now teaches writing at Southern Illinois University. He lives in Carbondale, Illinois, with his wife and family.

Topics to Consider

1) How does the novel's opening paragraph work to draw the reader into the story? How does the immediacy of the first-person narration affect the reader's involvement with Edgar and his story?

2) Edgar's mother doesn't even get up from the kitchen table when he is run over by the mail truck [p. 16]. Why is Edgar so forgiving of her, even though she abandons him and effectively kills herself with alcohol? Does she provoke any sympathy in the reader?

3) Edgar's father is a young white man from Connecticut who has come west in the hope of becoming a cowboy. Is it surprising that Edgar never meets or even tries to find his real father? Which characters take on parental roles in his life?

4) The reader is introduced to life at Willie Sherman in the chapter called "Edgar Gets It." Why are violence and sadism so casual here? What effect does the school have on Edgar's behavior? What changes does he make in order to survive?

5) Edgar makes daily use of the typewriter Art has given him. What does language do for Edgar? Why is it so necessary for him to write down what happens to him?

6) What does Edgar's friendship with Cecil mean to him? If thinking about and writing to Cecil have become some of Edgar's few emotional lifelines, what is the significance of the events that occur when he makes his visit to the juvenile detention center?

7) How does the landscape of the West affect the moods and meanings of the novel? Is there any significance to the fact that Edgar ends up in Pennsylvania, far from his Apache homeland?

8) How significant for Edgar's story is the fact that he is half Apache? What does the novel tell us about racial discrimination and its effect on Native Americans? How interested is Udall in bringing the reader's attention to the problems bequeathed to the Native American population?

For a complete Reading Group Guide,
visit www.vintagebooks.com/read

NOT THE END
OF THE WORLD

Author: Christopher Brookmyre

Publisher: Grove Press, 2002

Website: www.groveatlantic.com

Available in:
Paperback, 388 pages. $12.00
(ISBN 0-8021-3915-9)

Genre: Fiction/Intrigue/
Social Commentary

Summary

When LAPD detective Larry Freeman is given the assignment to monitor security at a B-movie film festival, he's expecting a walk in the park. But then he uncovers a strange connection between the festival and a convention of Christian evangelicals across the street—and he's launched headlong into confronting a cadre of terrorists who threaten to bring Southern California to the brink of apocalypse. The story, packed with a hilarious dialogue and skewering satire, is set amid a frenzied three-ring media circus featuring muckraking journalists, Bible-thumping radicals, and porn stars.

Recommended by: *The Times* (London)

"Perpetually in-your-face: sassy, irreverent, and stylish … [with] a high-octane sense of the absurd."

Author Biography

Christopher Brookmyre has worked as a journalist for several British newspapers and is the award-winning author of five novels, including ***One Fine Day in the Middle of the Night***, ***Quite Ugly One Morning***, and ***Country of the Blind***. He lives in Scotland.

Visit the author's website at www.brookmyre.co.uk

Topics to Consider

1) The author lives in Scotland, yet the story is set in Los Angeles. To what extent, if any, do you think his portrayal of the characters and LA culture reflects the way the U.S. is viewed by other countries?

2) Did you find the depiction of various groups—evangelists, film industry executives, militia groups, the FBI—accurate or stereotyped?

3) The action takes place in 1998-99, and reflects the anxiety of the time regarding the end of the millennium. How might your reaction to the book have differed had you read it when it was first published in 1998?

4) Waves play a prominent role in the story, both literally and figuratively. Discuss the metaphor of a wave to describe what Larry Freeman calls "the 1999 Syndrome" [pp.34-39]. Which cycle are we currently in? Are things getting worse, or are they getting better?

5) There are a number of products today marketed specifically to evangelical Christians, from "WWJD" bracelets to chocolate confections called "Testa-Mints", to the "sin-free sodas" that Steff finds at the Festival of Light [p.67]. Do you believe that people consume these products as a re-affirmation of their faith? Some other reason?

6) How are Steff's views of the Christian Family Channel's followers [p.82] shaped by his personal history and experience?

7) Luther St. John attributes his ill-fated presidential bid to media scrutiny [p.84]. Cite some other examples of media "spin" shaping public opinion.

8) Every one of the principal characters—Larry, Steff, Maddie, and Luther—has in common a history of trauma, pain and victimization, yet their personalities are quite different. How much do you believe our pasts shape our futures?

9) A key element of the story is the moral dilemma of sacrificing one life to save numerous others. What are your views? Are there circumstances that would change your point of view?

10) The book raises anew the question of why bad things happen to good people and vice versa. How would you answer this question, both before and after reading this book?

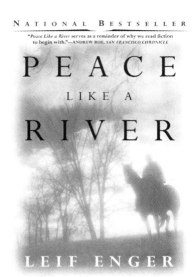

PEACE LIKE A RIVER

Author: Leif Enger

Publisher: Grove/Atlantic, 2001

Website: www.groveatlantic.com

Available in:
Paperback, 312 pages. $13.00
(ISBN 0-8021-3925-6)

Genre: Fiction/
Family/Faith/Americana

Summary

Set in the Minnesota countryside and North Dakota Badlands of the early 1960s, *Peace Like a River* is a story about one family's quest to retrieve its most wayward member. Reuben Land, the novel's asthmatic and self-effacing eleven-year-old narrator, recounts a journey riddled with outlaw tales, heartfelt insights, and bona fide miracles. Born without air in his lungs, Reuben is keenly aware of the gift of breath—and, by extension, the gift of life. Time and again, both gifts are bestowed on Reuben by his father, a gentlemanly soul who works as a school janitor and has the power—and faith—to bestow true miracles. But when Davy (Reuben's brother) kills two intruders who break into the Land home with evil intent, and then escapes from prison while his trial is in progress, events seem to have worsened beyond the aid of miracles. Or have they? For, once Reuben and his family set out to find Davy, the reader eventually witnesses rivers, plains, and city lights unseen by mortal eyes.

Recommended by: Tom Walker, *The Denver Post*

"Once in a great while, a book comes along that has such wonderful characters and marvelous prose, that you read it as much for the pure joy it offers on every page as to find out how it ends."

Author Biography

Leif Enger was raised in Osakis, Minnesota, and has worked as a reporter and producer for Minnesota Public Radio since 1984. He lives on a farm in Minnesota with his wife and two sons.

Topics to Consider

1) Begin your discussion of this book by recounting the major and minor miracles that occur throughout. What role do they play in **Peace Like a River**?

2) Does Reuben see Davy as a murderer, or as one who acted in self-defense? Does he want Davy brought to justice, or does he think justice has already been served? Discuss how the novel explores the idea of loyalty.

3) How does the Land family contend with the raw, uncivilized, and sometimes brutal landscape of rural Minnesota and the Badlands of North Dakota? Identify events or circumstances in which the novel's setting contributes to its elemental or mythic quality.

4) Besides the Sunny Sundown text, several other outlaw tales, literary allusions, biblical legends, and historical asides are offered—by Swede or by Reuben himself. Identify a few of these stories-within-the-story, explaining how each enriches or influences the main narrative.

5) Discuss the character of Jeremiah Land, Reuben's father—and the center of his moral compass. What are Jeremiah's strengths, as a person and a parent? Does he have any weaknesses? Why did his wife leave him, all those years ago? Explain how the novel's dual themes of familial love and ardent faith are met in this character.

6) Discuss the impact prayer has on Reuben, and how it transforms him. Reading this book, did you discover anything about the activity of, reasons for, or consequences of prayer?

7) What does the character of Roxanna bring to the Land family? What does she provide that the Lands had lacked before her arrival?

8) Much of this novel concerns the inner life of childhood: imagination, storytelling, chores, play, and school life. Discuss the author's portrayal of childhood. Do the children depicted here seem realistic? Why or why not?

9) Conclude your discussion by comparing and contrasting **Peace Like a River** with the traditional morality play—the symbolic drama (dating back to medieval times) based on the eternal struggle between Good and Evil.

THE RAVEN
WHO SPOKE WITH GOD

Author: Christopher Foster

Publisher: Singing Spirit Books, 2001

Website: www.SingingSpiritBooks.com

Available in:
Paperback, 148 pages, $ 12.95
(ISBN 0-9711796-0-3)

Genre: Fiction/Spirituality

Summary

Do we stay in our comfort zones or reach out and follow our dream? This is the question facing Joshua, a sensitive, vulnerable, but determined young raven who believes there is more to life than eating and playing. Despite the disapproval of his father, Joshua yearns to reclaim the long-forgotten relationship between ravens and humankind. Left all alone when his family is killed by cruel boys, he learns to listen to the voice of wisdom within himself as he overcomes his grief and fear and pursues his destiny. Some of his greatest obstacles are the most insidious, pleasurable ones!

Recommended by: NAPRA *ReView*

"Buoyant as the air through which the birds soar, the story lifts the heart and carries it, dancing lightly, all the way through to the end. This is a book you will read and then instantly think of ten friends to whom it must be lent."

Author Biography

Born 1932 in London, England, **Christopher Foster** is a retired weekly newspaper editor. He has worked as a reporter in the UK, Africa, New Zealand, and Canada, and lived in a spiritual community in British Columbia, Canada, before moving to Colorado.

SPECIAL OFFER: The author will gladly chat online or by telephone with any reading group that selects this book. Interested groups should contact the author through www.SingingSpiritBooks.com.

Topics to Consider

1) The book suggests that all life is one and we share a close kinship with animals. Is this idea foolish and unrealistic? If you think it is true, why? Do you have any personal experience to support the notion?

2) Joshua's mother senses that a special mission awaits one of her offspring. Do we all have a unique destiny in life?

3) While Joshua is alone facing darkness and despair, he suddenly becomes aware of an inner presence, a voice within himself that gives him hope and a sense of peace. Have you had an experience of this nature? Would you like to have it?

4) Edgar Allen Poe called the raven a "thing of evil," and some people do see ravens in this light. Now that you have finished Joshua's story, what do you think?

5) Joshua fights with his father because he thinks his dad does not understand him. Yet Ernie only wants to protect his son. Is he at fault? Could things have worked out differently for the two characters?

6) Describe the process of change and transformation that Joshua goes through in his journey. Do humans face the same challenges?

7) Joshua finds comfort and strength through his Aunt Esmeralda and others. Discuss the importance of mentoring. Are you a mentor to someone? Was someone a mentor to you?

8) Despite setbacks Joshua finds he cannot stop following his dream. How would you describe the "something" that will not let him give up?

9) How important is it to have a dream?

10) Do you have a greater appreciation for nature as a result of reading this book? Discuss the importance of nature in our lives.

11) Often, just when things seem to be going well, something happens that shakes Joshua out of his complacency or well-being. Why is this? Do you think true peace is possible in this life?

SHELTER FROM THE STORM

Author: Michael Mewshaw

Publisher: Blue Hen/Putnam, 3/2003

Website: www.penguinputnam.com

Available in:
Hardcover, 280 pages. $23.95
(ISBN: 0-399-14988-0)

Genre: Fiction/Suspense

Summary

The setting is a Central Asian country recently released from Soviet repression and now entering into a state of violent anarchy—where gunfire has become a natural part of the evening soundscape, where Muslims, Catholics, Jews, and Orthodox Russians live in uneasy proximity, and where the slightest miscalculation can be deadly. Zack McClintock thrusts himself into this world to discover the fate of his son-in-law, kidnapped by Islamic fundamentalists, and suffers an immediate disorientation. Widowed, feeling himself a failure as a father, and still haunted by a botched investigation in Switzerland years before, Zack asks himself not only why he has *really* come here but also who he really is. ***Shelter From the Storm*** is much more than a thriller. It is a vivid evocation of one man's physical and psychological disintegration and his ultimate transformation.

Recommended by: Robert Stone

"Mewshaw is one of the best American novelists, a master of plot and style at the top of his form. **Shelter From the Storm** *is a first-class read and a fine accomplishment."*

Author Biography

Michael Mewshaw has published eight critically acclaimed novels, including ***Year of the Gun,*** which became a John Frankenheimer film starring Sharon Stone, and half a dozen successful books of nonfiction.

Topics to Consider

1) In what ways does the setting of a chaotic former Soviet republic add to the atmosphere of suspense in the novel? What role does the setting itself—its landscape, history, and cultures—play in the story?

2) A lingering shade from the spirit world, Satan in human form, a victim of secret Russian chemical experiments, raised by wolves ... how would you explain the wolf-boy?

3) In considering his reasons for coming to Central Asia, Zack wonders in what measure his impulse to rescue was always just an excuse to wreak havoc. Much as he might argue that he was here only for Adrienne, he knew it was more than that. What are his other motives? In what ways is his past affecting his behavior?

4) Why does Zack identify so strongly with the wolf-boy? What does the wolf-boy remind him of?

5) What does the extremely odd cast of characters add to the novel? What does it reveal about the clash of cultures in Central Asia?

6) Why has Kathryn come to Central Asia? What does she hope will happen to her there? Why is she so attached to the feral child? Do you think she realizes her yearning to break through to this place and to deeper parts of herself? What role do her maternal instincts play in her decisions?

7) What role does love play in the major events of the novel? In what ways do the relationships between Adrienne and Fletcher, Tomas and Anna, and Zack and Kathryn drive the action of the story?

8) Zack wonders if things happened to him because of who he was. Or was he who he was because of all that happened? How would you answer these questions? Does our experience create our identity or does our identity create our experience? What does the novel seem to imply about these matters?

9) At the very end of the novel, how have events brought Zack to the brink of transformation? How do you imagine he will be changed?

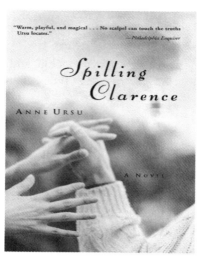

"Warm, playful, and magical . . . No scalpel can touch the truths
Ursu locates."
— *Philadelphia Enquirer*

Spilling
Clarence

ANNE URSU

A NOVEL

SPILLING CLARENCE

Author: Anne Ursu

Publisher: Hyperion, 2002

Website: www.HyperionBooks.com

Available in:
Hardcover, 288 pages, $22.95
(ISBN: 0-7868-6778-7)
Paperback (1/03), 288 pages, $12.95
(ISBN: 0-7868-8662-5)

Genre: Fiction/Human Behavior

Summary

What if you could suddenly remember everything that ever happened in your life? Would it be a blessing—or a curse? The answer is found in **Spilling Clarence**, a satisfying, witty, romantic, and tender novel. In the fictional town of Clarence, Minnesota, a break room microwave sparks a smoky fire at the pharmaceutical factory and triggers a massive chemical spill. Panic-stricken and paralyzed, the townspeople wait until the all-clear signal assures them everything's back to normal. Except that it isn't. Over the coming days, the citizens of Clarence fall under the spell of a strange and powerful drug that unlocks their memories. They become trapped by their own reminiscences: of love and death, of war and childhood, of family they've lost and sins they've committed.

Recommended by: *USA Today*

"Engaging—better than eavesdropping on a patient's tale to his analyst."

Author Biography

Anne Ursu was born in Minneapolis and graduated from Brown University. She has worked in the children's department of a major book retailer, as the theater critic for *City Pages* (Minneapolis), and as an arts writer for the *Portland* (Maine) *Phoenix*. She lives in Mountain View, California.

Topics to Consider

1) The people in the novel are affected by the deletrium in different ways. Age is a big factor in their reactions: how do children, adults, and the elderly react differently and why?

2) What do you think the point of the Davis and Dean Bookstore is? How does it function in the story? Is there any thematic relationship between the presence of a chain bookstore and a story about memory?

3) There are lot of minor characters whose stories are touched on in the novel (the manager, Lorna Hansen, Lilith, Ms. Plum). What do they add to the novel?

4) There are a number of points in the novel where the narrator breaks into the story and makes comments and addresses the reader. Why do you think the author chose that device?

5) Many novels consider the relationship between past and present. How is this novel different?

6) When Bennie sees Phil crying in his office, he thinks, "Our friendship does not encompass moments like these." What is the nature of their friendship? Phil is Bennie's only real friend in Clarence—why do you think that is? Why does Bennie let himself have a friend at all?

7) What attracts Susannah and Madeline to each other initially? What draws them so close after the spill?

THE SUNDAY WIFE

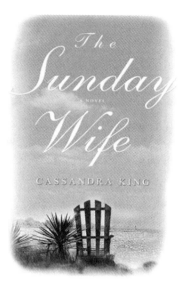

Author: Cassandra King

Publisher: Hyperion, 2002

Website: www.HyperionBooks.com

Available in:
Hardcover, 400 pages. $23.95
(ISBN 0-7868-6905-4)

Genre: Fiction/Women's Issues/
Friendship

Summary

Married for 20 years to the Reverend Benjamin Lynch, a handsome, ambitious minister of the prestigious Methodist church, Dean Lynch has never quite adjusted her temperament to the demands of the role of a Sunday wife. When her husband is assigned to a larger and more demanding community in the Florida panhandle, Dean becomes fast friends with Augusta Holderfield, a woman whose good looks and extravagant habits immediately entrance her. As their friendship evolves, Augusta challenges Dean to break free from her traditional role as the preacher's wife. Just as Dean is questioning everything she has always valued, a tragedy occurs, providing the catalyst for change in ways she never could have imagined.

Recommended by: *People*

"Rich [and] satisfying."

Author Biography

Cassandra King was born in Alabama, where she taught college-level English and writing. She now lives in South Carolina with her husband, author Pat Conroy.

Topics to Consider

1) What is a Sunday wife? What makes a "good" one? Consider whether or not Dean fits the bill, and explain your reasoning.

2) Who is the narrator and is this narrator reliable? Explore what the book would have been like if Ben had been the narrator. Consider how the story would unfold if one of the other characters were narrating.

3) What is the role of religion in *The Sunday Wife*? How does it frame—or anchor—the story? Share who you believe holds the book's moral center, and why.

4) Discuss the different social issues and dilemmas that King weaves throughout—like same-sex marriage, psychic healing, book banning and adultery—and examine why she uses them to tell this story.

5) Were you surprised at Dean's early admission that she and Ben don't share a bedroom? What kind of relationship does this lead you to believe that they have?

6) When Dean succeeds in cultivating a friendship with Augusta and Maddox, why isn't Ben ecstatic? Explore whether or not Augusta causes a rift between Ben and Dean. Is Dean and Ben's relationship already coming apart?

7) How are Dean and Augusta alike? What are your impressions of them? Thinking about Ben and Maddox, discuss their similarities and differences and what kind of men you think they are, and why.

8) On page 61, Dean and Augusta talk about fate vs. determination and choice. Share whether or not you believe, as Augusta does, that there are unseen forces that determine our fate. Why? How do Augusta's beliefs fit with what happens in her life?

9) Explore the turmoil Rich and Godwin's union causes the community. Why is Ben so upset about Rich and Godwin's union? Why was he so unsympathetic about Dean being attacked? What would you say to him if you were Dean?

10) Would you have given Augusta's note to her husband or hidden it from him like Dean did? Discuss why Dean does this and whether or not she was protecting Maddox. What are the consequences of Dean's actions? Why does Maddox get so angry when he finally reads the letter?

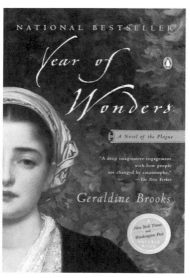

YEAR OF WONDERS
A Novel of the Plague

Author: Geraldine Brooks

Publisher: Penguin Books, 2002

Website: www.penguinputnam.com

Available in:
Paperback, 336 pages. $14.00
(ISBN 0-14-200143-0)

Genre: Fiction/Women's Issues/
History/Religion and Science

Summary

When an infected bolt of cloth carries plague from London to an isolated mountain village, a housemaid named Anna Frith emerges as an unlikely heroine and healer. Through Anna's eyes we follow the story of the fateful year of 1666, as her fellow villagers confront the spread of disease and superstition. As death reaches into every household and villagers turn from prayers to murderous witch-hunting, Anna must find the strength to confront the disintegration of her community and the lure of illicit love. As she struggles to survive and grow, a year of catastrophe becomes instead *annus mirabilis*, a "year of wonders."

Recommended by: *The New Yorker*

"A deep imaginative engagement with how people are changed by catastrophe."

Author Biography

Geraldine Brooks is the author of two acclaimed works of nonfiction, *Nine Parts of Desire: The Hidden World of Islamic Women* and *Foreign Correspondence: A Penpal's Journey from Down Under to All Over.* During eleven years as a correspondent for *The Wall Street Journal,* her beats included some of the world's most troubled areas, including Bosnia, Somalia, and the Middle East. Born and raised in Australia, Brooks lives with her husband, Tony Horwitz, and their son in rural Virginia. *Year of Wonders* is her first novel.

Topics to Consider

1) All of the characters in this novel have their failings and as a result they are all fully human. Are you surprised by the secrets Elinor and Michael Mompellion reveal to Anna about their marriage? How do they change your feelings about each character? Do they make each seem weaker in a way?

2) Setting aside the events near the end of the novel (which make it clear that one would be hard-pressed to find a redeeming quality in any of them), can you really blame the Bradfords for running?

3) How much of Mompellion's push for the quarantine had to do with the secrets he shared with Elinor? Did his own dark side and self-loathing push him to sacrifice the town? Or was he really acting out of everyone's best interests?

4) Keeping in mind that this story takes place a good twenty-five years before the Salem Witch Trials in Massachusetts, what is the role of the Gowdie women in the novel? What is it about these women that drives their neighbors to murderous rage? How does their nonconformity lead them to becoming scapegoats?

5) How would you explain Anna's mental and spiritual unraveling? What are the pivotal experiences leading up to her breakdown and her eventual rebirth?

6) Discuss the feminist undertones of the story. How does each female character—Anna, Elinor, the Gowdies, and even Anna's stepmother—exhibit strengths that the male characters do not?

7) In a story where the outcome is already known from the very beginning—most of the villagers will die—discuss the ways in which the author manages to create suspense.

8) Discuss some of the images you found most vivid—their importance to the story and to your own experience of reading it.

9) Can we relate the story of this town's extraordinary sacrifice to our own time? Is it unrealistic to expect a village facing a similar threat to make the same decision nowadays? What lessons might we learn from the villagers of Eyam?

HAS YOUR READING GROUP DISCUSSED....

Bel Canto
by Ann Patchett

Kitchen Confidential
by Anthony Bourdain

The Last Report On
The Miracles At Little No Horse
by Louise Erdrich

Visit **www.harpercollins.com/hc/readers**
to find reading group guides for these award-
winning titles and over 250 other books along
with tips on starting your own book club,
exclusive author interviews, and special
promotional giveaways available for your
reading group from HarperCollins.

HarperCollins*Publishers*

Looking for the perfect book for your reading group?

Look for this seal.

The **Ballantine Reader's Circle** is our esteemed collection of paperbacks, selected especially for reading groups like yours. When you see the BRC logo on the outside, you'll find our reading group guide inside, complete with discussion questions and author interviews. From contemporary fiction to vivid historical novels, acclaimed literary works to penetrating nonfiction, you'll find the kinds of books that provide great reading and create lively discussions.

Visit our Web site at at **www.ballantinebooks.com/BRC** to take advantage of our reading group resources and search our catalog of over 125 titles. And while you're there, **sign up for the Ballantine Reader's Circle e-newsletter and receive a chance to win free books**, monthly suggestions for your reading group, reviews of upcoming titles, exclusive author interviews, and much more!

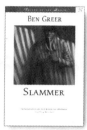

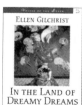

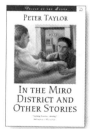

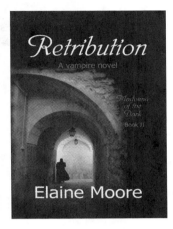

Looking for something new to read?

Paperbacks from Plume

Reading Group Guides, Excerpts, & Author Interviews
www.penguinputnam.com/guides

For more information e-mail:
PlumeMarketing@penguinputnam.com

Reading Group Guides Available from Plume

Dorothy Allison
Cavedweller
Trash

Julia Alvarez
How the Garcia Girls Lost Their Accent
In the Name of Salomé
In the Time of the Butterflies
Something to Declare
¡Yo!

Suzanne Berne
A Perfect Arrangement

Harriet Scott Chessman
Lydia Cassatt Reading the Morning Paper

Tracy Chevalier
Falling Angels
Girl with a Pearl Earring

Jennifer Chiaverini
The Cross-Country Quilters
The Quilter's Apprentice
Round Robin
The Runaway Quilt

Kevin Chong
Baroque-a-Nova

E. L. Doctorow
City of God

John Dufresne
Deep in the Shade of Paradise
Louisiana Power & Light
Love Warps the Mind a Little

Charlotte Fairbairn
God Breathes His Dreams Through Nathaniel Cadwallader

Rosario Ferré
Eccentric Neighborhoods
Flight of the Swan
House on the Lagoon

Maribeth Fischer
The Language of Good-bye

Karen Joy Fowler
Sister Noon

Jane Gardam
Flight of the Maidens

Linda Grant
When I Lived in Modern Times

Andrew Greig
The Clouds Above

Diane Johnson
Le Divorce
Le Mariage

Mira Kamdar
Motiba's Tattoo

Douglas Kelley
The Captain's Wife

Cathy Kelly
Someone Like You

Jamaica Kincaid
The Autobiography of My Mother

Hari Kunzru
The Impressionist

Pearl Luke
Burning Ground

Lee Martin
Quakertown

Bernice L. McFadden
Sugar
This Bitter Earth
The Warmest December

Toni Morrison
Beloved
Paradise
Sula

Bárbara Mujica
Frida

Joyce Carol Oates
We Were the Mulvaneys

David Payne
Gravesend Light
Ruin Creek

Ayn Rand
Anthem
Atlas Shrugged
The Fountainhead
We Are the Living

Cathleen Schine
The Evolution of Jane

David Schmahmann
Empire Settings

Darin Strauss
Chang and Eng

Katherine Towler
Snow Island

Augusta Trobaugh
Sophie and the Rising Sun

Salley Vickers
Miss Garnet's Angel

Jane Roberts Wood
Grace

Daniel Woodrell
The Death of Sweet Mister
Tomato Red

PLUME
A member of Penguin Putnam Inc.
www.penguinputnam.com

PENGUIN BOOKS and
THE GREAT BOOKS FOUNDATION

bring online discussion guides of the best classic
and contemporary fiction to your reading group

The Age of Innocence BY EDITH WHARTON (April 2003)
Age of Iron BY J. M. COETZEE (February 2003)
Anna Karenina BY LEO TOLSTOY
Carpenter's Gothic BY WILLIAM GADDIS
The Communist Manifesto BY KARL MARX AND FRIEDRICH ENGELS
Confessions of a Fallen Standard-Bearer BY ANDREÏ MAKINE
Dubliners BY JAMES JOYCE
Eichmann in Jerusalem BY HANNAH ARENDT
Equus BY PETER SCHAFFER
Frankenstein BY MARY SHELLEY (March 2003)
The Grapes of Wrath, Of Mice and Men, and *The Pearl*
BY JOHN STEINBECK (also available as a printed guide)
Ironweed BY WILLIAM KENNEDY
Jane Eyre BY CHARLOTTE BRONTË
The Last Days of Socrates BY PLATO
Libra BY DON DELILLO
The Little Disturbances of Man BY GRACE PALEY (April 2003)
Love in the Time of Cholera BY GABRIEL GARCÍA MÁRQUEZ
Midnight's Children BY SALMAN RUSHDIE (March 2003)
Moby-Dick BY HERMAN MELVILLE (February 2003)
Narrative of the Life of Frederick Douglass, an American Slave
BY FREDERICK DOUGLASS
The Odyssey BY HOMER (January 2003)
On the Black Hill BY BRUCE CHATWIN (January 2003)
The Pickup BY NADINE GORDIMER
The Prince BY NICCOLÒ MACHIAVELLI
The Procedure BY HARRY MULISCH
The Red and the Black BY STENDHAL
Seize the Day BY SAUL BELLOW
Thinks . . . BY DAVID LODGE
Two Lives BY WILLIAM TREVOR

guides available online at www.greatbooks.org and www.penguinputnam.com

USE YOUR BOOK SENSE™

Find your book group's next read among these
Book Sense™ Reading Group 76 picks from Penguin

#8

on the Book Sense™
Reading Group 76 list

Angle of Repose

by Wallace Stegner

0-14-016930-X
$13.95

RESOURCES

The Internet

Reading Group Choices Online — Includes a directory of over 575 guides available from publishers as well as more than 250 guides that can be printed directly from the site: **www.readinggroupchoices.com**

For new book information, reading lists, book news and literary events, visit **www.ReadingGroupGuides.com, www.generousbooks.com, www.BookSpot.com**, and **www.BookMuse.com**. Looking for reading guides for children? Visit **www.KidsReads.com**.

Publisher Web Sites — Find additional topics for discussion, special offers for book groups, and other titles of interest.

Algonquin Books of Chapel Hill — *www.algonquin.com*
Back Bay Books — *www.twbookmark.com*
Ballantine Books — *www.randomhouse.com/BB/read*
Broadway Books — *www.broadwaybooks.com*
Curbstone Press — *www.curbstone.org*
Doubleday Books — *www.doubleday.com*
Grove/Atlantic Press – *www.groveatlantic.com*
HarperCollins — *www.harpercollins.com*
Henry Holt & Co. — *www.henryholt.com*
Hyperion Books — *www.hyperionbooks.com*
Knopf Books — *www.aaknopf.com*
Little, Brown & Co. — *www.twbookmark.com*
Middleway Press — *www.middlewaypress.org*
Penguin Putnam — *www.penguinputnam.com/guides*
Picador — *www.picadorusa.com*
Random House — *www.randomhouse.com*
St. Martin's Press — *www.stmartins.com*
Scribner/Simon & Schuster — *www.bookclubreader.com*
Singing Spirit Books — *www.SingingSpiritBooks.com*
Sourcebooks — *www.sourcebooks.com*
Spinsters Ink — *www.spinsters-ink.com*
Steerforth Press — *www.steerforth.com*
Vintage Books — *www.vintagebooks.com/read*
Warner Books — *www.twbookmark.com*
Westcliffe Publishers — *www.westcliffepublishers.com*
Yale University Press — *www.yalebooks.com*

Newsletters and Book Lists

BookWomen: A Readers' Community for Those Who Love Women's Words, a bimonthly "bookletter" published by the Minnesota Women's Press. Includes recommendations, news about the book world, and articles for and about women readers and writers. Subscription: $24/yr. (6 issues). Contact:

books@womenspress.com or
Minnesota Women's Press
771 Raymond Ave.
St. Paul, MN 55114
(651) 646-3968

Reverberations News Journal, Rachel Jacobsohn's publication of the Association of Book Group Readers and Leaders. Annual membership including subscription is $20. Contact:

ABGRL
Box 885
Highland Park, IL 60035
(847) 266-0431
E-mail: *rachelj@attbi.com*

Books & Journals

Bibliotherapy: The Girl's Guide to Books for Every Phase of Our Lives by Nancy Peske and Beverly West. Published by DTP, ISBN 0-4405-0897-5, $13.95.

The Book Group Book: A Thoughtful Guide to Forming and Enjoying a Stimulating Book Discussion Group. Edited by Ellen Slezak and Margaret Eleanor Atwood. Published by Chicago Review Press, ISBN 1-5565-2412-9, $14.95.

Circles of Sisterhood: A Book Discussion Group Guide for Women of Color by Pat Neblett. Published by Writers & Readers, ISBN 0-8631-6245-2, $14.

Contemporary Multi-Ethnic Novels by Women Coming of Age Together in the New America by Rochelle Holt, Ph.D. Published by Thanks Be to Grandmother Winifred Foundation, $5 + SASE (6" by 8"). Write to 15223 Coral Isle Ct., Ft. Myers, FL 33919.

Family Book Sharing Groups: Start One in Your Neighborhood! By Marjorie R. Simic with Eleanor C. MacFarlane. Published by the Family Literacy Center, 1-8837-9011-5, $6.95.

Books & Journals (continued)

Literature Circles: Voice and Choice in Book Clubs and Reading Groups by Harvey Daniels. Published by Stenhouse Publishers, ISBN 1-5711-0333-3, $22.50.

Minnesota Women's Press Great Books. An annotated listing of 236 books by women authors chosen by over 3,000 women participating in Minnesota Women's Press Book Groups in the past 13 years. $10.95 + $2 s/h. (612) 646-3968.

The Mother-Daughter Book Club: How Ten Busy Mothers and Daughters Came Together to Talk, Laugh and Learn Through Their Love of Reading by Shireen Dodson and Teresa Barker. Published by HarperCollins, ISBN 0-0609-5242-3, $14.

The Readers' Choice: 200 Book Club Favorites by Victoria McMains. Published by Wm. Morrow, ISBN 0-6881-7435-3, $14.

The Reading Group Book: The Complete Guide to Starting and Sustaining a Reading Group by David Laskin and Holly Hughes. Published by Plume, ISBN 0-452-27201-7, $11.95.

Reading Group Journal: Notes in the Margin by Martha Burns and Alice Dillon. Published by Abbeville Press, ISBN 0-7892-0586-6, $16.95.

The Reading List: Contemporary Fiction, A Critical Guide to the Complete Works of 125 Authors. Edited by David Rubel. Published by Owl Books, ISBN 0-805055-27-4, $17.

Reading to Heal: A Reading Group Strategy for Better Health by Diane Dawber. Published by Quarry Press, ISBN 1-5508-2229-2, $10.95.

Talking About Books: A Step-by-Step Guide for Participating in a Book Discussion Group by Marcia Fineman. Published by Talking About Books, ISBN 0-9661-5670-6, $15.

Talking About Books: Literature Discussion Groups in K-8 Classrooms by Kathy Short. Published by Heinemann, ISBN 0-3250-0073-5, $24.

What to Read: The Essential Guide for Reading Group Members and Other Book Lovers by Mickey Pearlman. Published by Harper-Collins, ISBN 0-0609-5313-6, $14.

A Year of Reading: A Month-By-Month Guide to Classics and Crowd-Pleasers for You or Your Book Group by H. E. Ellington and Jane Freimiller. Published by Sourcebooks, ISBN 1-5707-1935-7, $14.95.

7 Easy Steps for Leading Book Discussions

1. Acknowledge your role as "facilitator" — not expert.

If it's your turn to lead the discussion, know that you are not expected to be an authority or expert on the chosen book. Your primary tasks are to open the discussion, keep it going, maintain a lively dialogue, and end the discussion on time. A great book discussion is the result of the thoughts and perceptions of a variety of different people.

2. Select a book that is discussible.

Not all books are discussible. Look for topics that are controversial, writing that is interesting, authors who are complex beings, writing that will stir emotions or stimulate thought and prompt the reader to talk about what they've read.

3. Tap available resources.

There are many sources for information. In addition to this book, look online to *readinggroupchoices.com* and *readinggroupguides.com* for guides you can print directly from these web sites. Publishers also make reading groups available online. Check the resources pages in *Reading Group Choices* for a list. You don't need to research authors or develop discussion topics unless you want to. Guides are available for hundreds of books in print.

4. Note your own response as you read.

Make notes as you read the book, highlighting or marking passages. What are your reactions, questions, or insights? Add the personal touch to your discussion. Share your thoughts during your discussion and invite others to comment.

5. Lay some ground rules.

After you've introduced yourself to the group, remind members of the ways they can contribute to the discussion:
a) Avoid "crosstalk" or talking over others.
b) Be respectful. Keep an open mind.
c) Try not to repeat what others have said. Speak up with something new or add to the previous comment.
d) Acknowledge that there is no right or wrong, just differences of opinion.
e) Be open to learn from others.
f) If you are outgoing, be careful to allow space for others to share their thoughts.

6. Call the question.

If you feel the group has begun to repeat itself, acknowledge your observation, ask for agreement if necessary, and pose a new topic.

7. Balance the discussion.

Invite quiet members to share their thoughts. Watch for the introverts who have something to say, but are having a hard time getting in a word.

BOOK GROUP MEMBERS

Name _____

    Day phone _____ Eve. phone _____

Name _____

    Day phone _____ Eve. phone_____

Name _____

    Day phone _____ Eve. phone_____

Name _____

    Day phone _____ Eve. phone_____

Name _____

    Day phone _____ Eve. phone_____

Name _____

    Day phone _____ Eve. phone_____

Name _____

    Day phone _____ Eve. phone_____

Name _____

    Day phone _____ Eve. phone_____

Name _____

    Day phone _____ Eve. phone_____

Name _____

    Day phone _____ Eve. phone_____

Name _____

    Day phone _____ Eve. phone_____

2003

JANUARY
wk	M	T	W	T	F	S	S
1			1	2	3	4	5
2	6	7	8	9	10	11	12
3	13	14	15	16	17	18	19
4	20	21	22	23	24	25	26
5	27	28	29	30	31		

FEBRUARY
wk	M	T	W	T	F	S	S
5						1	2
6	3	4	5	6	7	8	9
7	10	11	12	13	14	15	16
8	17	18	19	20	21	22	23
9	24	25	26	27	28		

MARCH
wk	M	T	W	T	F	S	S
9						1	2
10	3	4	5	6	7	8	9
11	10	11	12	13	14	15	16
12	17	18	19	20	21	22	23
13	24	25	26	27	28	29	30
14	31						

APRIL
wk	M	T	W	T	F	S	S
14		1	2	3	4	5	6
15	7	8	9	10	11	12	13
16	14	15	16	17	18	19	20
17	21	22	23	24	25	26	27
18	28	29	30				

MAY
wk	M	T	W	T	F	S	S
18				1	2	3	4
19	5	6	7	8	9	10	11
20	12	13	14	15	16	17	18
21	19	20	21	22	23	24	25
22	26	27	28	29	30	31	

JUNE
wk	M	T	W	T	F	S	S
22							1
23	2	3	4	5	6	7	8
24	9	10	11	12	13	14	15
25	16	17	18	19	20	21	22
26	23	24	25	26	27	28	29
27	30						

JULY
wk	M	T	W	T	F	S	S
27		1	2	3	4	5	6
28	7	8	9	10	11	12	13
29	14	15	16	17	18	19	20
30	21	22	23	24	25	26	27
31	28	29	30	31			

AUGUST
wk	M	T	W	T	F	S	S
31					1	2	3
32	4	5	6	7	8	9	10
33	11	12	13	14	15	16	17
34	18	19	20	21	22	23	24
35	25	26	27	28	29	30	31

SEPTEMBER
wk	M	T	W	T	F	S	S
36	1	2	3	4	5	6	7
37	8	9	10	11	12	13	14
38	15	16	17	18	19	20	21
39	22	23	24	25	26	27	28
40	29	30					

OCTOBER
wk	M	T	W	T	F	S	S
40			1	2	3	4	5
41	6	7	8	9	10	11	12
42	13	14	15	16	17	18	19
43	20	21	22	23	24	25	26
44	27	28	29	30	31		

NOVEMBER
wk	M	T	W	T	F	S	S
44						1	2
45	3	4	5	6	7	8	9
46	10	11	12	13	14	15	16
47	17	18	19	20	21	22	23
48	24	25	26	27	28	29	30

DECEMBER
wk	M	T	W	T	F	S	S
49	1	2	3	4	5	6	7
50	8	9	10	11	12	13	14
51	15	16	17	18	19	20	21
52	22	23	24	25	26	27	28
1	29	30	31				

INDEX BY SUBJECT/INTEREST AREA

INDEX BY AUTHOR

INDEX BY AUTHOR

(continued)

INDEX BY GENRE

Nonfiction

Fiction

INDEX BY GENRE

Fiction (continued)

Reading Group Information
@ Your Fingertips

✓ Looking for other ideas about what to read?

✓ Want to know if a guide exists for a particular book?

✓ Need to print a guide in a hurry?

✓ Want title information from previous print editions of *Reading Group Choices?*

✓ Seeking guidance on how to start (and run) a book group?

✓ Want to order additional copies of *Reading Group Choices?*

For years, *Reading Group Choices* has been a primary resource for book groups. Visit us online for full profiles of over 300 recommended titles plus information on reading discussion guides that are currently available — from large publishers and independent presses. **Reading Group Choices Online** is an industry-wide, central resource.

What's New

Browse Guides by Subject

Search Available Guides

Tips on Starting
A Book Group

Guidance for
Group Leaders

Visit Reading Group Choices Online

www.readinggroupchoices.com